AN IGBO CHILDHOOD

AN IGBO CHILDHOOD

Samuel D Ibekwe

ATHENA PRESS
LONDON

Acknowledgements

I should like to express my sincere gratitude to the following people without whom this book would not have been written:

To Judy Havrlik, the primary inspiration for this book, and also for editing it.

To Dr Gilbert Chigbo of Enugu, Nigeria, who rigorously checked the names and dates and provided the anecdotes to lighten the story.

To Danielle Vandervliet who was responsible for the final editing of this book and for the translation into French.

To Yohana, my wife, for her patience and encouragement.

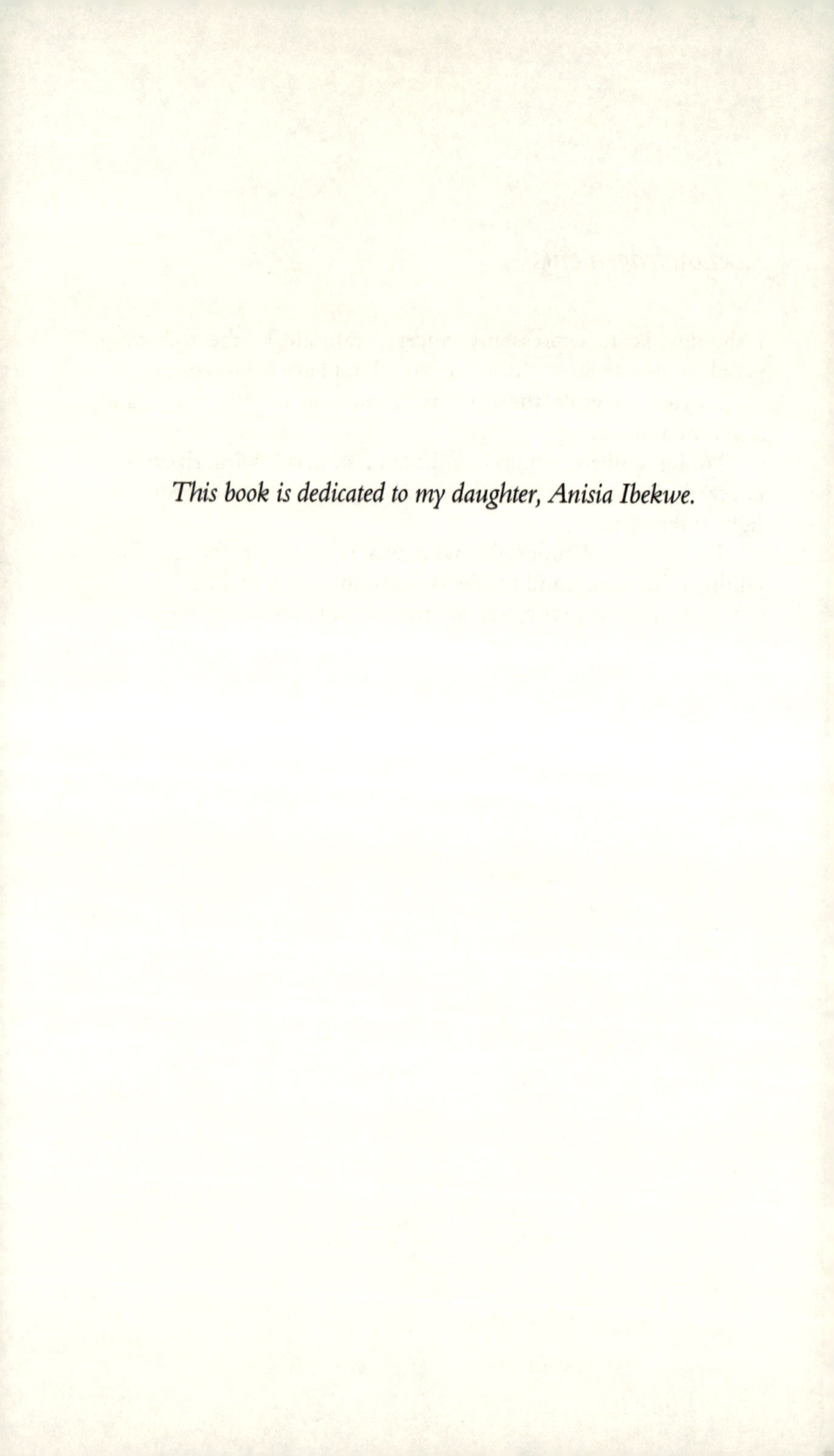

This book is dedicated to my daughter, Anisia Ibekwe.

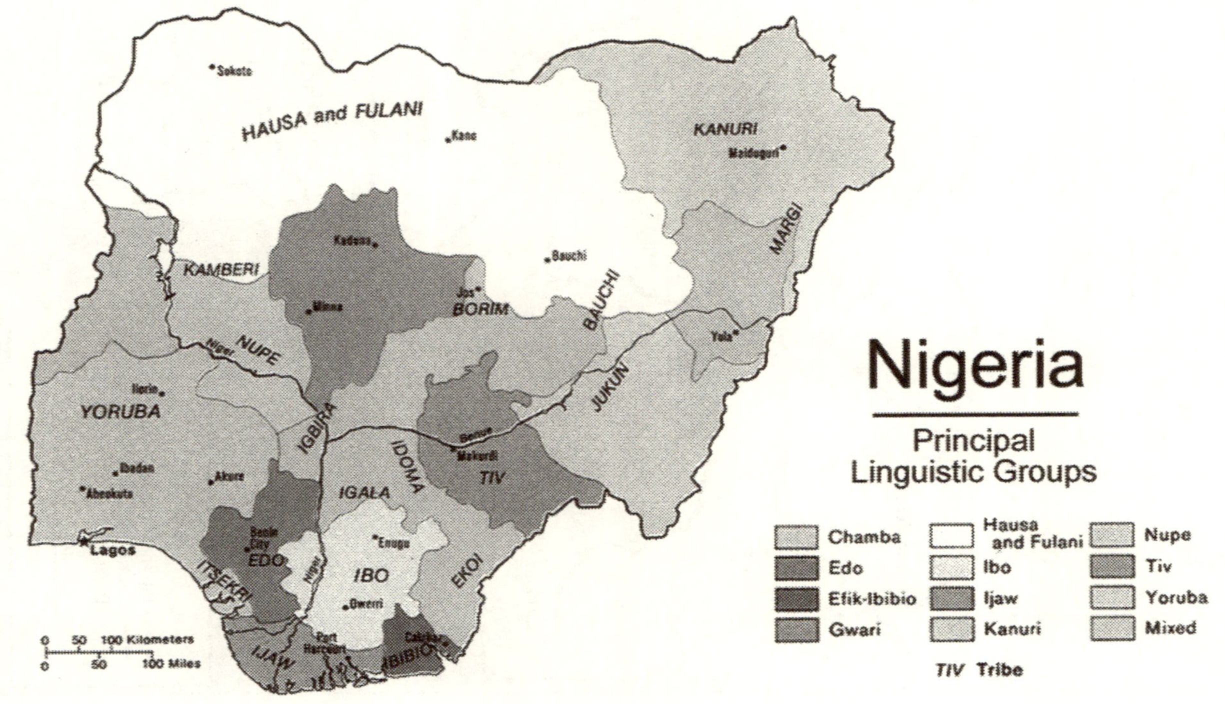

Nigeria
Principal
Linguistic Groups
HAUSA and FULANI
Sokoto
Kano
KANURI
Maiduguri
KAMBERI
Kaduna
Minna
Jos
BORIM
Bauchi
BAUCHI
MARGI
Yola
JUKUN
NUPE
Niger
Ilorin
YORUBA
IGBIRA
IDOMA
Benue
Makurdi
TIV
Ibadan
Akure
Abeokuta
IGALA
Benin City
EDO
Niger
IBO
Enugu
EKOI
Lagos
ITSEKRI
Owerri
Port Harcourt
IJAW
IBIBIO
Calabar
0   50   100 Kilometers
0   50   100 Miles
Chamba
Edo
Efik-Ibibio
Gwari
Hausa and Fulani
Ibo
Ijaw
Kanuri
Nupe
Tiv
Yoruba
Mixed
TIV Tribe

NIGERIA
N
MALI
NIGER
Tahoua
Bimi Nkonni
Naimey
Dosso
Illela
Maradi
Zinder
Gouré
Diffa
Kaura Namoda
Katsina
Nguru
Sokoto
Bimin Kebbi
Gusau
Kano
Damaturu
Dutse
Pokiskum
BENIN
Kandi
Kontagora
Zaria
Kaduna
Bauchi
Biu
Ndali
Wawa
Jos
Gomba
Parakou
Kisi
Minna
Bida
Abuja
NIGERIA
Yola
Shendam
Jalingo
Ogbomoso
Ilorin
Baro
Lafia
Bali
Ibadan
Osogbo
Lokoja
Makurdi
Wukari
Abeekuta
Akura
Keja
Benin City
Enugu
Banyo
Lagos
Sapele
Asaba
Awka
Bamenda
Tibati
Porto-Novo
Owerri
Umuahia
Bafoussam
CAMEROON
Bight of Benin
Warri
Aba
Calabar
Nkongsamba
Port Harcourt
Uyo
Oron
Kumba
Buea
Douala
Yaoundé
Malabo
Isla de Bioko
Mbalmayo
Gulf of Guinea
Kribi
Sangmelima
Bight of Biatra
Ebolowa
Campo
MAP KEY
Beta
Byern
International Boundary
Acalayong
Railroad
National Capital
River
State Capital
Cocobeach
GABON
0   100   200 Kilometres
0   200   200 Miles

Introduction

I started writing this story as a result of a dinner party in Brussels in 1999. We were at a party with friends when someone recounted little bits of their childhood experience in Wales in the United Kingdom. At the end of the story, a lady sitting next to me asked what my childhood had been like and I found myself telling a story of growing up in a small colonial town in Nigeria at about the time the Second World War was ending. When I had finished my story, the same lady spoke to me again.

'Have you written any of this down?' she inquired.

'No,' I said.

'You should damn well hurry up and do so before you forget the details. I am sure your account is special; it will never be lived again in Nigeria or anywhere else.'

And so this story is a recollection of an African childhood in the 1940s in British-administered, pre-independence Nigeria. It tells what growing up was like for an Igbo child in South-Eastern Nigeria in the 1940s and the impact of missionaries and British rule on Igbo society. With hindsight, this was in fact a period of transition from British colonial rule to Nigerian independence, twenty years later, in 1961. In many ways, it was a glorious and innocent childhood that has long disappeared from Nigeria and from other parts of the world. The wretchedness of the African child that is so omnipresent today was unknown to us in those days. We may have been poor and exposed to all manners of preventable diseases, but we felt secure and happy.

I have written this story for my only daughter, Anisia, and for my grandchildren. It is a record of a life they will never know – a life they can only read about and marvel at! I hope it brings immense joy and wonderment to all that read it.

The earliest memories of my childhood must be of playing in the narrow unpaved sand path that separated our house at 86 Clifford Road, Aba, from our neighbour's at 84 Clifford Road,

Aba, in colonial Nigeria. I played at being a fireman or a laundry man with other children and I must have been between three and four. Years later, I would learn that kids of my age in Europe and Asia also wanted to be firemen and train drivers.

But the most vivid memories of my childhood are of that early morning in January 1942 in Aba, Eastern Nigeria. I was five and a half years old. It was to be my first day at school and I was to be sent to the local elementary school at Christ the King School, Aba – a Catholic missionary school barely two hundred metres from our house. In 1942, I was the only surviving child of my parents. My younger sister Veronica had died of dysentery in 1940. My father owned a thatched-roof house at 86 Clifford Road, in the 'non-European' residential area of Aba. My mama did not take me by hand to school. Instead, I was carried overhead, screaming and crying, by a cousin, Alfred, who worked for my father as a sales assistant at our family's general stores in Aba. Before that, I had spent most evenings in the previous year learning my ABC at home under the supervision of a local teacher. It had not occurred to me that one day I would leave home to go to school. Childhood was carefree and happy.

Papa owned a shop at 33 Asa Road, a shop he had rented from Chief Manuel-Brown of the Rivers Province. In those days, Asa Road was a wide boulevard, lined on both sides by trees. Indians, Lebanese and Greeks owned the principal shops in downtown Asa Road. The few Nigerians who owned shops in Aba at that time were the greats such as Remy Okoro of Arondizuogu, and M C Obiora who was the Chairman of Aba Urban District Council on which my father served. European-owned shops such as Paterson and Zochonis (PZ), United Africa Company (UAC) and others, were on Factory Road, near the European quarters on the other side of town, beyond the railway station.

We had a maid, Bridget, who had come from our village of Akokwa to be trained by my mother in the art of cooking and looking after a home; in short to prepare Bridget for marriage. Bridget subsequently left two years later to get married and was replaced by my Auntie Maggie, who looked after me for most of the next five years. There were other maids in our house and they looked after the other children born to the tenants of our house.

All the children spent all day playing together at improvised roles – as policemen, train drivers or laundry men. Going to school would take me away from my friends to an alien community of teachers and kids from another section of town.

So, on that fateful January morning in 1942, my mother accompanied by Alfred who carried me, forcefully but gently, on his head, to the mission school at Christ the King Catholic School, Aba, where I was unceremoniously deposited. I remember sobbing for quite a while and then seeing other youngsters also with red eyes who had suffered the same fate. We all subsequently settled down and I do not remember anything further about that day.

Apparently, behind me in the queue that day was a certain fair-skinned child called George Spiropoulos. We were to become very close for the rest of my life. In December 2000, I recounted this story to 'Georgie' in Lagos and he confirmed that he was the child behind me in the queue on that school registration day.

Family Roots

My Grandparents

I did not know either of my paternal grandparents. My father's mother and father were long dead before I was born. By contrast, I knew both grandparents on my mother's side. My grandfather on my mother's side was called Onyenakala and his wife, my grandmother, was called Agaranma. Onyenakala was a tall, dark, handsome man who owned a lot of land. He died when I was about seven or eight, but I vividly remember what he looked like.

My grandmother by contrast was a small, compact woman, with fair skin and a sharp nose. She had very penetrating eyes with pale pupils. She came from the nearby town of Achina. Her successors in Achina today, such as the Nwizugbo family of Achina, regard us as blood relations, too close for marriage. Agaranma and Onyenakala were the pillars of their village, Umuokwara, in Akokwa. Agaranma had three children, Njanma, the eldest, my mother, later baptised as the Catholic Theresa; Joseph (Joe) the only son and Margaret (Maggie), my aunt.

I have been close to all three all my life. When Grandpa Onyenakala's brother died, he was obliged by local custom to 'marry' his brother's widow – a sort of social security – and she bore him three other children, a girl and two boys. The custom in Igbo land was that a brother took on the widow of his brother and looked after her as his wife. I suppose that made for family solidarity. Widows living on their own had a difficult time in Nigeria in those days.

Agaranma became a highly valued source of ancient values, ideas and knowledge, until the end of her life. She knew which herbal doctor to contact for different illnesses. A good example of this is illustrated by the following event that actually happened to me. I was old enough to remember it very clearly.

I think I was about eleven years old and I had a severe attack of malaria that had degenerated to jaundice. It was in December and Christmas was not far away. Everything was dry, with a lot of dust brought down south by the Harmattan wind from the north. I felt a lot of nausea every time I smelt cooking oil, especially groundnut oil. Red blood cells of people suffering from malaria are destroyed by the malarial parasite and the debris clogs up the liver. The liver in turn is no longer able to filter quickly enough, so that most of the destroyed red blood cells come out through urine as a yellow-brown liquid. My eyes and skin were yellow. My urine was yellow. Western medicine for malaria at this time was mainly Paludrine and Nivaquine. They had been administered to me at the Aba General Hospital and I was not getting any better. My parents, who had already lost three children some few years earlier, were terrified and in despair. Everyone was terrified as I lost weight every day and had no appetite. My father decided to try local, or what was called native medicine.

We left Aba for Akokwa, our village of origin. As soon as we got home to Akokwa my grandmother was called in and my mother, in tears, told her I was passing away.

From what I was told, she immediately went to a witch doctor to find out whose evil spirit was trying to kill me. In addition, she knew the most effective herbal doctor in the area and promptly sent for him. Our medicine man disappeared all afternoon into the nearby forest to collect leaves and roots from local trees. He insisted that nobody followed him, presumably to protect his knowledge. At sunset, the herbal medicine man returned from the forest. It was dry and dusty. The air was so dry that I think I began to hallucinate in the heat. My grandmother introduced the herbal medicine man. He took out his cowry shells and threw them on the floor and made some incantations. My parents were now too westernised to make anything of the proceedings, although they were still believers. My grandmother was our guarantor for the occasion, making sure that the medicine man was not a quack that would poison me with his potion. Grandma had never converted to Christianity and was in a sense still in contact with local customs and medicines. Grandma had confidence in this medicine man or *Dibia* and he dared not let her grandson die.

At the end of the incantations, the herbal doctor produced a

75ml beer bottle stuffed with roots and leaves. From his other bag he produced a sheaf of green leaves that he had recently cut from the forest. Fresh palm wine was poured into the bottle mixture of roots and leaves. It was now about 5.30 p.m. In half an hour or so it would be dark. I was to drink a glassful of the extract before going to bed, and after that three times per day. I was also required to bathe with hot water and extract of the leaves every morning. Around 10 p.m., as the owls stopped singing, everybody in the village would be in bed. I slept in a hot and badly ventilated room, tossing all night.

At daybreak, at approximately 5.30 a.m., I remember getting up from my bed and feeling relatively conscious of who I was, and that I had been ill with fever all night. I went out to pee in the nearby bush. My urine that until that morning had been a deep yellowish-brown seemed to lighten in colour to a pale yellow. I developed an appetite and asked for food. For the next ten days, I drank my potion three times a day and bathed in the herbal bath twice a day. My urine lightened in colour every day and by the tenth day, it was water-white. The white of my eyes also cleared. I was cured, and with my subsequent training in science, I can categorically affirm that my cure from acute malaria and jaundice was by herbal medicine and not the pills from the general hospital in Aba. Years later, when I was sixteen and was down again with malaria at my boarding school at King's College, Lagos, I sent home for my herbal bottle from Akokwa. A cousin who had travelled more than 450 km by road to get it to me delivered this to me three weeks later. By the way, the taste of this medicine was awful – more like a sour beer extract of sawdust, but it worked! We never found out what it was and I dare say this medicine man is no longer alive. Have we lost his cure or do his grandchildren know what plants and roots he used?

Agaranma was a pillar in my life when we visited Akokwa. She was the only reference on local customs – on what was permitted and what could or could not be done. She knew all about local rules and taboos and where you could or could not walk in the village, to avoid evil spirits or simply avoid poisoned footpaths. On market days, *Ahia Orie*, we would accompany her to the market held every four days (the Igbo week). There, she would exchange her home-grown potatoes (*egbede*) for palm oil or goat meat, etc.

People traded with cowry shells and huge bronze money tokens called *icong*. Or simply they exchanged goods by barter. Sophisticated items like cloth, kerosene and tobacco were brought from the townships like Aba where merchants like my father had access to them by importation from Europe. Nearly all my childhood holidays were spent in our parental village of Akokwa, away from the township of Aba. The reasons were both rational and mundane. My parents wanted me to be familiar with our roots and local customs at Akokwa. Aba, which was no more than 70 kilometres away from Akokwa, was regarded as foreign, owned by the Ngwa people, a subdivision of the Igbo tribe. The truth in fact was more ordinary. The Ngwa people feared all these Igbo people from the Igbo hinterland – the red-earth countryside – migrating to their city, Aba.

Almost all my Christmas holidays until I was twelve were spent in Akokwa, and my preferred place was my grandmother's cottage. Her house was old-fashioned, with a carved wooden door for entry and a big courtyard in front of it. Behind were various vegetable farms from which she gathered all the food she cooked for us. Chickens and goats ran around all day. For drinking water, she would make me travel at dawn on foot, to a distance of about four kilometres with my aunts, to an underground spring water source at Idenmili. For cooking or washing, we made do with rainwater that was collected from the thatched roof of her cottage. Inside Granny's three-bedroom house, we slept in one room on rattan beds around a central fire. A fire was always lit when we visited for the Christmas break in December.

Cold winds from the Sahara Desert would bring the Harmattan or *Uguru* to the Igbos. A fine red-ochre dust covered everything, hence the name *aniocha* or red lands for the Igbo heartland.

Granny had a granary where maize, yam and various spices were stacked in parallel ladders to hang and dry and provide seedlings for planting for the next season. Commodities for immediate consumption were hung from the ceilings of Granny's cottage. And so, at an early age, I was able to appreciate the differences in texture and taste of new yam and old yam. Old yam was more leathery and fluffy. When roasted on an open fire and soaked in freshly made palm oil it gave a better taste than fried chips. So many fruits and vegetables hung from the ceiling that up to this day I am amazed the house never caught fire. Those ceilings were used in much the same way as people hung out garlic to dry in the south of France.

Once a year the village mason redecorated Granny's house. Essentially, this involved making a fluid paste from the red earth that is abundant locally. This was used to paint every wall and floor of the building, so that it looked new. The carved wooden door had the motifs on it regularly redone with the blue and yellow dyes available locally from the indigo plant. She spent her days farming her food crops and looking after my father's house, that was about two kilometres from her house. Granny was the only person my father could trust to look after his property and when she died in 1978, we estimated she was about 92 years. She specifically asked not to be buried by a Christian priest, but in accordance with her animist beliefs.

My Father – Gabriel Mmeje Ibekwe

My father was called Mmeje Ibekwe. He added the Christian name Gabriel after his conversion to the Catholic faith. I did not know or meet any of my father's family except for my father's sister, and also Chief Mathias Okafor. Mathias Okafor is, as I write this, still alive and aged about 90 years, and has outlived all his immediate relations. He is in fact my father's first cousin. In later years I was to see a great deal of Chief Mathias Okafor, as he was regarded and treated as my father's elder brother and the head of our extended Okafor-Ibekwe family. I saw my father's sister for the first time when I returned from studying at university in England in 1965. I was never to see her again until my father's funeral in 1986.

My father, Gabriel Mmeje Ibekwe, was born in Akwu village in Akokwa. Akokwa in those days was in Mbanasa Local County District which included Arondizuogu. Our District headquarters was Orlu. Mbanasa included Osina, Urualla, Uga and is in the red lands of the Igbo heartland. During the Biafra War that started in 1968 and ended in 1970, Akokwa provided one of the two airstrips used by the Biafran army. The other airstrip was at Ulli. That is how central Akokwa is in the Igbo heartland.

Gabriel Ibekwe started life as a tax collector for the British Colonial Administration in Orlu District of Owerri Province, Eastern Nigeria. By the time he died in 1986, he had been made a chief of his beloved Akokwa.

After a brief period as a tax collector, Gabriel Ibekwe moved to the city of Aba where he opened a *shed*, or shop, and traded in textiles imported from Europe. Aba was and still is a very busy town for traders. He lived most of his life in Aba, but always went home to Akokwa, his village of birth, three to five times a year.

Akokwa is a small town of about 100,000 people in the old Orlu District of Owerri Province, Eastern Nigeria. My father's major achievements were made in Akokwa, where he was rewarded with the chieftaincy title, *the Ihemeghonye of Akokwa*. (He who has not suffered would never be wise.) My father's parents were peasant farmers in Akokwa, although from his records, he claims they came from a royal household. My father was a remarkable man who kept copious diaries of all his transactions. He married my mother at the Christ the King Church, Aba, in 1935 in what he described as a glittering ceremony. They had eight children, of whom three died. In later life he married two other women, Rosalind and Laeticia, as was the custom in the 1950s. He felt by then he was a successful and important member of the community and one way of showing off his success was by taking more wives. All his friends, including my uncle, had done so and they encouraged him to follow suit. He would end his life with sixteen children by my mother, Rosa and Laeticia, and would spend all he had to give us all a good education.

From my father's hand-scribbled notes, written on a blue exercise notebook, we learn that he was born to a poor farmer couple, Okorafor Ibekwe, in Akwu village, Akokwa. There was one other child, a girl, who was my father's younger sister and who married into the neighbouring town of Osina.

A self-taught man, my father had reached grade two in elementary school in Akokwa when his father died. Subsequently, his mother brought him up alone. After school he would go into the neighbouring forest to gather firewood which he sold the next day to pay his school fees and to help his mother. This way he made another two years in school to reach the fourth grade at his elementary school. According to the records written in 1953 by my father, he says:

Umudieleke was the leading household and largest family in Akwu village of Akokwa. Dieleke was the head of a family that had twenty-seven chiefs and he, Dieleke, owned thirteen houses. A row had broken out in the distant past, between Dieleke and the chiefs of a neighbouring town (probably over land). The neighbouring village declared war against Dieleke and his twenty-seven chiefs. Dieleke and his chiefs were massacred and their houses seized. The Dieleke dynasty was thus abolished and incorporated into today's village of Akwu in Akokwa.

Chief Dieleke himself had two sons, Dim and Umeonye,

from the same wife. Dim, one of the sons, later produced an only son, Ezenwa. Ezenwa in turn also produced only a son, Agharagwo. Agharagwo in turn had two sons – Agbanero and Ibekwe.

Ibekwe gave birth to a son Mmeje, my father, who subsequently converted to Catholicism as Gabriel Mmeje Ibekwe. Agbanero gave birth to Mathias Okafor, my uncle. With very little education, my father joined the British Colonial Administration as a tax collector in Orlu. He soon found he could not make ends meet and moved to Aba to trade. He died on the thirteenth of February 1986 and we reckoned he was 80 years old, with 1906 as the year of his birth. In his lifetime, Gabriel Ibekwe was a Councillor, Aba Township Municipal Council; chairman, Market Committee, Aba Urban District Council; secretary, African Transporters Union, Aba; co-founder and First President, Akokwa Town Union, Ideato LGA, for 11 years; co-founder and first Chairman, Akokwa Town Union, Aba branch; member of first Nigeria Electoral College (1960) for Eastern Nigeria.

Gabriel Mmeje Ibekwe was one of the earliest to participate in representative democratic elections under British rule. He was elected councillor for Aba township and became chairman of the Housing and Market Committee, arguably the most important committee.

He was responsible for allocating shops, *sheds*, in Aba township market and also responsible for allocating new premises for constructing new houses in Obohia, the extensions to Aba township.

He was so rigorous in his performance that it was later said by my father's assistant at the council that the Englishman responsible for administering Aba Urban Council pleaded with my father to give himself a piece of land on which to build a house. And that is how he got the house at Obohia Road. Photographs of the Aba Urban District Council show him in a well-tailored suit, with other councillors, in the company of the visiting British Resident Officer of Owerri Province.

As secretary of the Africa Transporters Union, he became involved in local politics and thus got linked to a Nigeria-wide national party, the National Council of Nigeria and the Cameroons (NCNC), led by Dr Nnamdi Azikiwe. The local Aba hero of that party was Mbonu Ojike from Arondizuogu, a radical who had studied in the United States. As the fight for independence accelerated in the 1950s, Ojike urged a boycott of British goods by Nigerians as a way of putting pressure on the British. His slogan was 'Boycott the boycottables'. In other words, 'do not import from Britain any goods you could do without'. Other local stalwarts of the NCNC living in Aba included the barristers Jaja Wachukwu and Raymond Amanze Njoku, both of whom ended up as federal ministers in Lagos in the first Nigeria Federal Government of Tafawa Balewa of 1961. Aba and Onitsha were the key cities of radical Igbo politics in the 1940s. They were also the richest, and central to the two wings of Igbo culture, the so-called *high* Igbo (Onitsha) and the *low* Igbo (Owerri). The two wings had different intonations for the same words.

Mbonu Ojike visited Aba in the 1940s to launch the anti-imperialist campaign to 'boycott the boycottables'; urging people not to patronise imported goods as a way of putting pressure on the British. We, as kids, did not know what he was talking about. What I remember was his magnificent, long, open Buick convertible car. It had a multiple horn system that impressed all of us when it swept past on Asa Road, on its way to a political rally. According to Professor William Okefie-Uzoaga, Professor of Finance, University of Nigeria, Nsukka, who died in 1992 and who delivered my father's obituary address in Akokwa in 1986,

Gabriel Ibekwe pioneered and remained the most prominent leader of the Akokwa community in Aba. He developed and guided the Akokwa community at Aba into a formal union. His next step was to broaden urban unions in Onitsha, Calabar, Port Harcourt etc. by the formation of a Federal Union of Akokwa Communities at home and abroad, throughout Nigeria. This meant the integration of the urban unions with the larger rural bodies at Akokwa. The rural bodies were stratified in informal traditional associations, clearly independent and naturally suspicious of each other. To understand the leadership qualities of Gabriel Ibekwe, one must appreciate the skill, the patience and the ingenuity with which he used the Federation of Akokwa Town Unions to break the domestic isolation of communities. The result was the emergence of a large integrated union bound together for a common purpose. And this was achieved without injury to any member of the component groups and personalities.

The inauguration of the Federation of Akokwa Town Unions was scheduled to take place in the grounds of St Barnabas Catholic Church, Akokwa. The priest in charge of the premises thought that this new organisation that would accommodate non-Christians and Christians of other denominations would contaminate his flock. He therefore disapproved both of the gathering and the inauguration of the Union in the premises of his church. Undaunted, Mr Ibekwe led the members out of the Catholic Mission premises to Obi Okoli's palace, and the Federation of Akokwa Town Union was inaugurated there within the hour. The year was 1937. Mr Ibekwe was elected the first president-general of the Union, with Mr E E Munonye as secretary and Godfrey Ukachukwu as treasurer. After his first five-year tenure of office, Mr Ibekwe was unanimously re-elected for a further five-year term. He served the federation for twenty years (1937–1957), eleven of which as its president. One could rightly ask why, that out of a population of some 50,000, a town continued for two decades to demand the leadership of one man. The answer is not easy but could be found from Ibekwe's strategies of leadership – democracy, consideration of the poor and public accountability of officers. He successfully pioneered a written constitution that skilfully incorporated what was desirable in our tradition with what was salubrious in the minds of the emerging urban elite of the 1930s.

His achievements for Akokwa were many and varied. Under Mr Ibekwe's leadership, the unity of this town, its name and therefore its history were put to a serious test in the 1950s. An attempt was made to change the name of Akokwa. After all persuasions to drop the change had failed, Mr Ibekwe mobilised the town to resist. A Public Commission of Inquiry appointed by the Eastern Region Government ruled in favour of the wishes of Akokwa people. The victory strengthened Ibekwe's leadership.

My father's other achievements included the construction of Akokwa Town Hall. As president of the Akokwa Union, my father was responsible for the construction of a town hall on the principal road axis of the town. He was in regular communication with government ministers. Ibekwe exchanged correspondence with state and federal ministers of the day, for instance with Dr K O Mbadiwe, Federal Minister of Communications, resident then at 3 Liverpool Road, Apapa. Dr Mbadiwe came from Arondi-zuogu and had been elected by Mbanasa council to which Akokwa belonged. In a letter dated October 20, 1961, the minister regretted that he did not see Ibekwe, president of Akokwa Town Union, when he, Dr Mbadiwe, addressed the Akokwa people on October 1, 1961. The minister also recorded that he had not seen Ibekwe at the meeting of September 28, 1961 in Enugu as part of a delegation that was to meet the then Eastern Regional Governor, Dr Mike Opara, for the first time. These meetings were to mobilise Arondizuogu and Akokwa people for the forthcoming Mbanasa Regional Election. Only Dr Elechukwu and one other were present at this meeting and the minister expressed his deep disappointment at the poor turn out of Akokwa representation. This must have been during the quarrel on whether our little town should be spelt as Akaokwa or Akokwa. This quarrel had Akokwa's two first PhDs, Dr Elechukwu Njakar and Dr William Okefie-Uzoaga respectively, pitted against each other in a bitter struggle. Akokwa town was also divided.

The spelling *Akokwa* won the day over *Akaokwa*. What a truly stupid issue to divide a town that had no water and no post office! The quarrel over the spelling drama nearly cost the town its post office as will be seen in the section 'Akokwa Post Office'.

The secretary of the Town Union during this period was a Mr I E Uchendu, with Simon I Anyikwa as deputy president to Ibekwe. History has it that Anyikwa, who was probably wealthier than Ibekwe, resented playing second fiddle to Ibekwe and so sided with those who wanted the spelling of the town to be *Akaokwa*.

Akokwa Post Office

A committee headed by Ibekwe put out tenders in May 1961 for the construction of a post office in Akokwa. After much wrangling and postponement due to whether the post office was to be called *Akaokwa* or *Akokwa*, Ibekwe wrote a memorandum on August 30, 1962 in which he said the following:

Went to Port Harcourt (Akokwa Town Union) and was told that the post office would not be built because of the dispute in the spelling of Akaokwa as against Akokwa. I told them to give the post office to me to build for them.

On the day I went to Onitsha asking them to come and register their names for the forthcoming election, they received me with my vice-chairman and president and secretary, quite well. They made a strong protest about the misspelling of Akaokwa instead of Akokwa. They continued saying that if this thing is not mended, that they are not coming to vote. In the speech that I made to them, I strongly promised them that the one letter error would be amended when I resumed my office as president. Ditto for Port Harcourt and Aba.

At the first Akokwa Town Union Meeting held after the election at Akokwa, this question of name came out for discussion and all the people adopted that they (the town) should be called by their father's old name which is Akokwa.

At the meeting of 1st July 1962 it was reported by the youths that people are still spelling the name of Akokwa wrongly and it was decided that as from 1st October 1962, anyone found still mis-spelling the name of Akokwa must pay a heavy fine. This resolution was to be published in the *Eastern Nigerian Outlook* and *Morning Post*, and to write to the Post Master General, to change the Post Office stamps.

At the last meeting of Post Office Committee, I asked the secretary if he has done the publication according to the decision of the meeting. He said that he had no chance. Then I told him to see that the resolution made at the last meeting be recorded out and given to the vice-chairman, Mr Anyikwa, who will publish it according to the resolution at the meeting. I also asked the secretary to draft a letter and forward it to the post master general to change the Akokwa Post Office stamps to their real name.

What is striking about this memo is how well written it was, and the sense of executive duty and authority that my father felt he was obliged to carry out for the people who had elected him as president. His secretary and vice-president were probably not laughing, as he ploughed on with what he saw as his duty! In addition to the above, the style and quality of English were surprising. This memo was also written on a typewriter, which suggests he either had a secretary at 86 Clifford Road or that he did it himself. I learned how to type during my vacations from King's College, Lagos in 1953 and 1954 on this old Imperial typewriter.

On September 19, 1964, the Federal Minister of Communication, the Hon Olu Akinfosile, finally officially opened the Akokwa Post Office. A formal address of welcome was presented and signed first by Chief & Venerable S N Okoli, MBE, the Obi of Akokwa. The second to sign was Gabriel M Ibekwe, President, Akokwa Town Union, followed by S I Anyika, Vice President and then Daniel Nwokeji, Treasurer and Dr W Okefie-Uzoaga.

The Police Station in Akokwa

This was formally opened on October 25, 1962 during Ibekwe's reign as president of the Town Union, in the presence of many dignitaries including Dr E Njaka, MP in the Eastern House of Assembly and Chief P Okoli, President Akokwa Chiefs. The Nigerian police force today properly staffs the police station.

My Mother – Theresa Njanma Ibekwe

On the 22nd of January 1933, Gabriel Ibekwe received a letter from a Sister M Joseph of the Holy Rosary Convent, Onitsha, Nigeria, British West Africa and it read:

Dear Sir
In reply to your letter asking for your intended wife, Njanma, to be admitted to the day school, I beg to state we do not accept girls of her age to begin a.b.c. We have a vocational school where she can learn to read and write and count as well as to do other useful things. I am enclosing a prospectus and I am reducing the terms to 15 shillings monthly. With the hope that you will give the girl a chance to become a good, useful wife and mother.
Wishing you God's blessing.

Yours sincerely,
Sr M Joseph

The prospectus that accompanied this letter read in part

The Missionary Sisters of Our Lady Of The Holy Rosary, founded by the Most Rev. Dr Shanahan, C.S.Sp. for the Vicariate of S. Nigeria, have established a Boarding and Day School at Onitsha, W/S. They have for object, the salvation and sanctification of the souls of the women and children of Southern Nigeria, particularly of the Catholic girls confided to their care and the pagan girls who wish to embrace this religion. One of the principal means employed to help in the establishment of the One True Church in Nigeria is a High Class Educational System to prepare the girls religiously, intellectually and physically for their great destiny as children of God. The Educational Authorities have highly approved of our Primary and Vocational Schools.

The Vocational School – This is established for the preparation of young girls for Christian Marriage.

Subjects

- Religious Doctrine, Moral Science
- Singing and Liturgical Chant
- Hygiene and Sanitation, Care of Infants (theoretical)
- Elementary knowledge of English, Arithmetic, Penmanship
- Citizenship
- Plain and Fancy Needlework, Dressmaking
- General care of house. An improved system of native cookery
- European methods of utilising native products
- Fees – 15/- per month, paid in advance

Fifteen shillings per month was a stiff fee and probably represented half or more of my father's profits as a trader in Aba in 1933. And so, my mother, having been betrothed to my father according to native laws and customs, set out to be trained at the age of eighteen, as was the term in those days, to be a wife and mother, at a convent school. My uncle, Chief Mathias Okafor, claims even today that it was he who found my mother, then a willowy young thing, probably sixteen years old, on her way to fetch water. He quickly alerted Gabriel Ibekwe of what he had seen and from then on, a marriage was agreed between the Ibekwe and Onyenakala families in accordance with Igbo customs. My mother proceeded to the Holy Rosary convent in Onitsha for the next eighteen months. There are no certificates to show what she actually achieved. There is little doubt however, that by the time mother left the convent in Onitsha she could just about speak English. I doubt if she learnt enough to be able to write her name. I never saw her do that in her lifetime. My mother was by now a beautiful young lady who had converted to Catholicism and had been baptised as Theresa. You had to be a convert if you wanted to get on. She was probably no more than eighteen years old.

On leaving the Catholic Convent in Onitsha by 1934, my father sent my mother to a finishing school in Aba, to prepare her for life as a future wife and mother. She was sent to live with a Catholic matron in Aba, a family from Arondizuogu who lived at the lower end of Clifford Road, Aba. It was the Amakwe family – Mr Robert and Mrs Susanna Amakwe. They were already well known in Aba and Mrs Amakwe taught my mother how to look after the home. My mother lived with her adoptive family from 1934 until her marriage to my father in November 1935. My father certainly saw her from time to time, but they were not allowed to be together alone, before marriage. This fitted in well with both the teachings of the Catholic Church and Igbo culture. Their marriage took place in 1935 and the picture of the couple in 1935 shows a dapper Mr Gabriel Ibekwe in a three-piece striped suit with a white pocket handkerchief, black suede shoes and a homburg hat at his side. Mother was clothed in a beautiful white dress, high-heeled shoes with white stockings and a string of pearls around her neck. Her hair was covered in white lace and she wore a silver ring on her wedding finger. She looked much younger than my father – a good fifteen years less, I would think. All the items they wore were imported from England. The photograph that survives shows an elegant couple, stylishly dressed in a manner reminiscent of a middle-class professional family in England of the 1930s.

According to a record by my father in a ledger that we recovered, he notes on the very first page:

> 24 November, 1935. On the above-mentioned date, I was married at Christ the King Roman Catholic Church, Aba Township. Service – 8 o'clock a.m. High Mass; refreshments 1.30 p.m. The function was very good. G. M. Ibekwe.

The official marriage certificate states:
Nigeria: The Marriage Ordinance, Section 24 – Form E Schedule 1:
Certificate of Marriage: no 35 of 24/11/1935.
Marriage celebrated in the Catholic Church at Aba in Nigeria. Date – 24/11/1935.
Name of Husband – Gabriel Ibekwe – Bachelor – Trader – Father's occupation – Farmer.
Name of Wife – Teresa Njanma–Spinster–Domestic work – Father's occupation – Farmer
Marriage at Catholic Church Aba before me, – (signature) Eugene Groetz.
Witnesses: Robert Amakwe and Susanna Amakwe.

The Family Ledger

Our father kept a record of all the important events in his life in a leather bound ledger – details of births, baptisms, first days of school and deaths.

And so my dear mother gave birth to eight children over a period of twenty years. I suppose that was normal at the time, but nevertheless rather traumatic. Five of us have survived to today with families and different professions. Given our start-off position, I think both Papa and Mama would be very proud of us today. Unfortunately, they are no longer around to see what we have achieved or share in some of our success, or in their grand-children. Of the five of us who survived, one child has a doctorate in chemistry, another is a medical doctor and a specialist in tropical medicine in Nigeria; the third runs a car-hire company in the USA. One of the girls is a senior secondary school teacher in a government college in Nigeria and the second girl is a senior primary school teacher in Nigeria.

I remember very well the three children who died. Veronica died of dysentery; Louis and Michael apparently died of yellow fever. According to Dr John Ibekwe, my younger brother, only yellow fever killed rapidly in those days. Louis and Michael died within one month of each other (May and June 1944). The symptoms of yellow fever are similar to those of malaria, but yellow fever kills much more quickly than malaria.

Father was totally destroyed with grief. I was now the only child (eight years old), and my parents went everywhere with me for fear that whatever had killed their three other children would strike again. I remember seeing Dr Solanke, the medical doctor in charge of the General Hospital Aba, come to our thatched roof house at 86 Clifford Road, Aba. Papa wanted to know if we were living in dangerously unsanitary conditions that had caused the deaths. He did not go for a local fetish doctor to tell us whether we were cursed. In many ways, he was already quite Cartesian, using reason and logic to face the most difficult period of his life. Dr Solanke passed our house, as healthy and safe for habitation. Next was a visit by a Catholic priest who sprinkled holy water around the house to keep off evil spirits.

Growing Up in Aba

Aba was founded around 1920 as a small market town and was developed by the British into an administrative centre. It became an important road and rail hub soon afterwards and an important regional market that also manufactured basic necessities such as soap and palm oil. The population was estimated at about 120,000. Today, it is probably one million! In 1929, Aba women rioted against taxation and arbitrary use of local people as chiefs for indirect rule.[1]

Aba was the key hub linking the Igbo hinterland with the important merchant port of Port Harcourt, 60 kilometres to the south and traditionally inhabited by the Calabari and Ijaw peoples. Founded in 1921, Port Harcourt was named after the British Colonial Secretary of the time, Lewis Harcourt. To the east of Aba was Calabar, a seaport on the Cross River. From Calabar all manner of goods were smuggled into Aba from Cameroon, Equatorial Guinea and Fernando Po. Aba was, and still is, the meeting point for traders of the old Eastern Nigeria. People came from Calabar and Ibibio regions; from Mbammiri and the Rivers Region of Port Harcourt and traders from as far away as Bamenda in the Cameroon.

The Catholic Mission in Aba

Christ the King Church, Aba was and probably still is, one of the four top Catholic dioceses in Eastern Nigeria. The first is Onitsha where the archbishop lives. The second is Umuahia, with the cathedral. Owerri must be the third because they have a seminary there. Christ the King Church and school largely formed me. For me and for my friends, the mission was the centre of our lives. The Holy Ghost fathers formed our characters and we revered

---

[1] *The Columbia Encyclopaedia, Sixth Edition 2001*

and sometimes feared them. The catechist, an Asaba man who was also the interpreter from English to Igbo at mass, lived in a mission house in the same compound as the revered fathers. As a result, he was also holy. At least that is what we thought. He spoke slowly and in deliberate terms. If he caught you running when you should not be, or shouting, he would dress you down in such a manner that you were afraid for your life. It was better he never saw you, not even to compliment you.

The Rev Father E J Groetz was one of the early missionaries to come to Igbo land and was in charge of the Aba diocese. Father Groetz was the architect of the Roman Catholic church at Aba, in the form of Christ the King Church, and gave it both a kinder-garten and a renowned elementary school. A Holy Ghost father from Alsace in France, he spoke and understood Igbo.

Everybody called him Father Grace. He was a heavily built man who looked like a giant to us kids. He always seemed to be sweating and everybody was terrified of him. He always had a peculiar smell, not of alcohol and not the sort of body odour you associate with the poor in Africa. It was a dry sort of smell which we called 'the white man's smell' – a kind of wood smoke smell. We assumed the smell came from the incense that they wafted at mass every day.

The mission had two other Reverend Fathers – the Rev Father Stiegler, also French from Alsace, and Father J Hampson, a young, burly Irishman who joined them around 1945. Father Hampson played football and rode a powerful motorcycle, a Harley Davidson, maybe. We would not have known in those days. The whole of Aba heard whenever he roared out of the mission, down Asa Road, at full throttle. It was an incredible sight to see this priest mount his bike in his long white cassock and take off, looking like a crazed woman. He would be on his way to some cool fresh air by the Imo River, which crossed Aba at the hilly top of town. Father Hampson took over the running of the two schools and successfully organised a junior football team, St Joseph's, in which George Spiropoulos, my Greek–Nigerian boyhood friend and myself played.

I liked going to Father Groetz for confessions because he gave you a lighter penance. Father Stiegler – the small bearded one –

on the other hand, gave you a stiffer sentence, a whole rosary sometimes.

The school football ground was the biggest in Aba and the height of the week was a football match on the school football pitch after evening prayers on Sunday, usually between two major football clubs in Aba.

High Mass on Sundays was at 8.30 a.m. Children's mass was at 7 a.m. Father Groetz waited at the door for the 8.30 a.m. mass and shut the door promptly at 8.30. God help anyone who was late! I will never forget the scene one Sunday when the mother of my friend, George Spiropoulos, arrived late on her elegant lady's bicycle, dressed in a beautiful European dress with huge necklaces around her neck, late for mass! George's mother was very beautiful, the only African woman in Aba married to a white man in the 1930s. Spiropoulos, her Greek husband, worked as an engineer at the soap factory owned by Paterson and Zochonis in Aba. I had also come late to mass that day and the main door to the church had been shut. Father Groetz, in faltering Igbo, berated Mrs Spiropoulos and asked her who she thought she was, arriving late for mass. How dare she come late to church, dressed scantily in a provocative manner and wearing disgraceful jewels! He ripped the jewellery from her neck and threw it to the floor. Mrs Spiropoulos did not react or panic. She just stood there and took it all in. As children, we were convinced that Father Groetz fancied George's mother. She was his devil, his temptation.

When Father Groetz died in 1948, the town's shops and market were shut down as a sign of respect and church bells rang out all day. He was buried in a cemetery in the church grounds and for years people said his ghost came out at night and terrified people nearby. Someone must have believed it, because many years later, metal chains were erected around his grave which is still revered and looked after!

I was a choirboy at Christ the King Catholic church and had the honour of climbing up to the hanging gallery at the back of the church from which the choir sang. We sang in Igbo, English, and Latin. It was glorious, especially at midnight mass on Christmas Eve. At midnight on Christmas Eve, the only bright light around would be the light from the church. Several dozen

Tilley lamps would light up the interior and exterior of the church, giving it a sort of heavenly glow. To receive communion at midnight mass, we were required not to have eaten any food from about 6 p.m. that evening. This meant that we were very hungry come midnight. That, combined with being awake at midnight, the heat and the intoxicating aroma of incense at church, meant that you were in a state of being 'high' and you saw 'angels' floating through the church ceilings!

The Roman Catholic mission, a stone's throw from our house, was the centre of my childhood. I was already in the pre-elementary school there. The mission had a vast expanse of forest where we played hide and seek. It had three large football pitches and at weekends all life revolved around it. My friends were largely people I knew from the school or who lived on our road.

All life revolved around the mission. I started school in January 1942 in class Infant 1 and moved to Infant 2 in 1943. The two years of pre-elementary schooling were worrying. I had left home and my playmates, and now had to make friends with new kids. We wore pretty blue and white check shirt and white shorts, but no shoes – we could not afford them. School for the infant classes started at 7.30 a.m. That meant getting up at about 6 a.m. Mother would then boil water to wash me; feed me, mostly with *akamu* (maize porridge) and *akara* (fried black-eyed bean balls). These would be purchased the same morning from an itinerant Hausa man selling them by our street. By the time I was dressed it would be about 7 a.m. and mother would then take me to the mission school by hand, walking, to make sure I was there before 7.30 a.m. when the doors shut. We carried our black slates with chalk in our small raffia bags. It was always a big crisis when someone dropped his or her slate and it shattered. The school blackboard was part of the school wall that was painted black. This was refurbished by rubbing it with the leaves of the indigo plant, to give it a dark hue. Every morning we were required to recite our times tables, and if you made a mistake, you were made to stand in front of the class and your fingers were caned with a ruler. You were also caned if you came late to school in the morning. In the afternoon when it was very hot inside the school, we did catechism classes outside under the big mango tree by the church. You could not be promoted to a higher class if you failed your religious examination.

One of the major activities in the morning was physical exercise, in which we lined up outside on the playing field and did press-ups. I remember vividly wading through lush green grass that was wet with morning dew. We hated that because we were barefoot and in shorts, and wet grass feels very cold in the morning to an African child. There was of course the constant fear of snakes. These were usually green grass snakes that we subsequently learnt, as older children, were not dangerous.

The other major activity at school was to produce on the Monday of every week, our week's collection of palm kernels for the war effort. The British colonial administration required every child at school to donate a cigarette can volume (Capstan cigarettes) of palm kernel every week. This was collected all over the country and shipped to England where it was converted into margarine. That was my effort for the Second World War. It was damn hard work, looking for fallen palm fruits in the bushes around Aba. My mother sometimes had to buy palm kernels from the local market to make up my quota. The climax of the year was a Mass in mid December – some saint's feast day. A High Mass would be said in the morning and after that all the kids at the school would remain behind with their parents. Father Groetz or Father Stiegler would announce in English that school results would follow after the mass. The catechist, the Asaba man, would translate this into Igbo in a singsong accent. This is where the end of the year school report would be read out. Children who had passed their exams would be promoted and those who failed would repeat.

There would be something like 500 parents and kids in this church hall. The headmaster of the school, Mr John Edemanya, an Onitsha man, would preside over the proceedings. Each class teacher, starting from Infant 1 to Standard 6, would read out loud from the pulpit of the altar, in alphabetical order, the names of the kids that had been promoted to the next class. When your class was announced, you had to listen very carefully for your name. If a name after yours was called without you hearing your name first, then it meant you had failed. It was terrible. You would hear children screaming with pain and fear as they realised that they had failed. Everybody in the church knew they had failed. Their lives were ruined. In truth, did it really matter then? I do not think so. Those friends who were not academically inclined went on to live fulfilled lives as successful businessmen in Nigeria.

Those who passed their exams heard their names read out loud and clear to the congregation. They screamed with joy. Their parents beamed with pride and you got three pence to buy yourself some coconut, or ground nut or *moi moi* (black-eyed beans pudding). You could not buy *suya* (fried meat on spikes) which we really craved for because it was sold mostly at night by Hausas. Besides, our parents feared that we could develop a liking for suya, and subsequently become thieves, stealing money from our parents to assuage our desires! I spent the afternoon after the results with my friends in the European quarter of town.

Behind 33 Asa Road, at the Market Road entrance, there was a very nice and salubrious residential bungalow of two-stories, inhabited in those days by upper class Nigerians. The family was none other than that of my light-skinned classmate from school, my Greek–Nigerian friend, George Spiropoulos. They used to live at Hospital Road – he, his Greek father, Nigerian mother, his elder brother Charles and his beautiful elder sister, Victoria. His father died, I believe, in the 1940s, and his mother remarried. His mother married non other than the chief medical officer of Aba General Hospital, Dr Femi Solanke, and they lived just behind our shop.

Other prominent locals in the Aba of the 1940s included the Allwell-Browns from Rivers Province who owned a pharmacy in Milverton Avenue; the Wadibias who owned Emy cinema in Hundred–Foot Road and Barrister Jaja Wachukwu. They all lived in the well-planned residential quarters for African professionals in Park Road or Pound Road. Roads had gutters in which water ran continuously in order to stop mosquito larvae breeding. The gutters had grass verges as borders. Fruit trees like guava trees, oranges, mangoes, etc., were planted next to the verges, making Aba an overall green and pleasant town. There were two open-air cinemas in Aba, the Rex cinema, owned by a Lebanese, and Emy cinema owned by Ngwa-born Wadibia family. Both cinemas were still there in the year 2000. Emy Cinema still operates as a cinema, with the day's programme written on a blackboard in white chalk and shows beginning at 9.00 p.m. Films at Emy Cinema are no longer cowboy westerns but romantic dirge in Hindi from the Indian sub-continent. Rex cinema, near Aba town hall, has been converted into a gigantic parking lot for buses. So much for the work my father and his contemporaries did for Aba in their days at the town hall!

By the time I got to Standard 3 elementary in 1946 (five years from the start), I knew a few of the teachers and actually liked them. One was a man who had come back to Aba after the war. He was a tall, handsome man who had a very distant look in his eyes. Perhaps he had had some peculiar experience in Burma. The Nigerian contingent of the British Colonial Army had been sent to Burma. Many, according to my father, had lost their arms trying to pick up booby-trapped watches that had been dropped by the Japanese. I cannot remember his name now, but he was a marvellous man and also a devout Catholic. He had been in the army and had been demobilised when the war ended. He came to school in his army boots with hobnails and walked as if he was marching. That must have been around 1945, when the war ended. We were not affected by the war as children. Papa certainly knew about the war, as he clearly recorded in his ledger in 1940:

> 24th August 1940. On the above date, Louis Ibekwe was born (at) about half past five in the evening, at (the) African Hospital Aba. It was on Saturday and the same day and very hour, we are having war practice about German war at Aba.

We knew that the war had ended in 1945, when I was nine years old. There was a mini-riot along Asa Road, the main thoroughfare in Aba. Ex-service soldiers demobilised from their campaign in Burma were back in Aba, and somehow the authorities had not arranged for their homecoming. Apparently, a few soldiers went into the market place and wanted some food. Of course the locals could not care less that they were heroes returning from serving their country and the British Empire. The market traders wanted to be paid for their goods and when the ex-servicemen refused, a fight ensued. Nobody was shot, but there was a good fight that the traders won.

By 1946, aged ten, Benjamin Maduka 'Bengie', Georgie, Henry, Vincent, Augustine and a few others were my best friends. We all attended Christ the King Roman Catholic School and we formed a group, a gang that moved from one neighbourhood to another after school hours. Georgie's father, the Greek, had died several years before. Georgie's mother had married the chief medical officer of Aba General Hospital, Dr Solanke, a Yoruba man. They had a new set of children who differed from Georgie and his Greek-father-parented brother and sister. The new and old families got on very well and it was remarkable to see how they lived. In those days, it was all accepted as normal – a Yoruba chief medical officer in an Eastern Nigerian town married to an Igbo woman. I knew this to be the case because Dr Solanke had moved his family to the two-storey colonial house at the back of 33 Asa Road. Our shop was at 33 Asa Road, and Georgie and his family literally lived just behind our shop. After school, I would go to Papa's shop to help him in selling cloth and lamps, etc., and later in the afternoon I would escape to Georgie's 'upstairs house' to play with him. These must have been very happy moments in my childhood, because many years later, I still dreamt of going to this house to play and plucking paw-paw fruit from nearby trees in their garden.

Some of our favourite pastimes after school, especially during the Christmas holidays, were to go to the better part of town; the European quarters near the railway station. Here you had magnificent colonial houses with huge fruit gardens and alpine type trees called Casuarina. They have thin pine needle-like leaves and moved in the wind to provide refreshing air in the hot dry Harmattan season, just before the rains. The only trouble with these trees was that snakes also liked living in them. We would climb lots of fruit trees – mango, sour-sup, false apple trees – and pluck their juicy fruits to eat. Occasionally, the European occupant of the house would come out to chase us or send his dog after us. We would run like hell and jump over the walls. Our band would spend a whole day in the European quarter because it was less crowded and had playgrounds. Years later, in the late 1960s, I returned to Aba to visit my parents. I made the same journey on foot, from our house at 86 Clifford Road. I crossed the Catholic mission into Asa Road, through to Milverton Avenue and Factory Road to the European quarters, the railway station and the 'rest house', a distance of about four kilometres, to try and recapture this innocence and beauty. There was still some atmosphere left in the 1960s. There were still the unmistakable smells of my childhood. By the late 1990s, it was all gone except, miraculously, the golf course, that has survived.

Health conditions in the 1940s and 1950s were precarious and it was a miracle we survived. Running water was available but only at Ehi Road (400 metres away) or as far as St Michael's road, a kilometre away in the residential area inhabited by African lawyers or clerks. Our house was at the edge of the African part of town, inhabited by upwardly mobile traders. We were part of what was called 'ABA N° 1'. These were the first trader settlers of the town under British rule, like Remi Okoro, C C Green, reputedly the richest man in Aba, and others like my father. The planned part of Aba town was full by the late 1940s. It was planned like the typical mid-west towns of the United States.

Roads ran parallel to one another in a north/south direction, dissected by roads running east to west. Each road had a drainage gutter next to it with a hedge of grass on either side of the road. Further up north, in the smarter part of town such as Pound and Park Roads, there were trees along the roadside.

By the year 2000 the grass had largely disappeared but some of those beautiful trees can still be seen in Pound Road. There were many new arrivals to Aba in the late 1940s and early 1950s. These were village folk coming to Aba to be apprenticed to merchants like my father, to learn how to trade. We had five or six people like that living with my parents. They were mostly relations of my father and they worked at all the minor jobs such as cleaning the compound, looking after our shop at 33 Asa Road and washing the car when we acquired one briefly in the late 1940s. Some also would go on long journeys from Aba to Lagos, the capital. Their journey would take them from Aba to Onitsha where they crossed the River Niger to Asaba (there was no bridge over the Niger River at this time). From Asaba they would travel through Warri, Benin and arrive in Lagos, the capital, after twenty-four hours in a truck. Their mission was to buy merchandise which had just arrived from overseas. Lagos was the only port functioning in those days. They would buy cloth, cutlasses, rubber sheets – you name it. Any goods in demand in the East were purchased and resold in Aba to people coming from even further afield as Bamenda in the Cameroons and Calabar in the far eastern corner of Nigeria. Aba was the commercial crossroad of Eastern Nigeria.

Among these apprentices were some beloved people like Alfred, who carried me to school on my first day in 1942, Richard, Francis, Ohaba, etc. These people made up our family even though they worked for my father. At the end of the apprentice period, which could last up to ten years, they left our household and were helped to set themselves up in business. I believe my father gave them about £100 sterling each. That was a lot of money in those days. The heartbreak as these people left our home was terrible. I had known them all my life. Years later, some of them would come back to introduce their wives and children, with great pride, to me and my brothers and sisters. Strangely, the nature of the relationship never altered. They saw themselves still as people who had served my father as their *Oga*, or boss. Some of these former apprentices of my father wanted their own pieces of land to build on. The Aba Urban District Housing Committee, chaired by my father, allocated land to them and other new arrivals to Aba, outside the municipal boundaries. Unfortunately, they had to live in the unplanned part of town, Ama Mmong without street names or pipe borne water. There was no electricity in our part of town. There was electricity in the European part of town because there were factories like the Paterson Zochonis soap factory where Georgie's father was the chief engineer.

You had to go to Port Harcourt to see electricity in ordinary people's homes. For me that came true when I spent a brief holiday with my cousins, the Emeghebos, in the garden city of Port Harcourt in 1948. At our house, in 86 Clifford Road, Aba, our family occupied the front part of the building in four bedrooms, with a large sitting room where my father met visitors. There was no electricity, and lighting was from kerosene lamps or, if you were well-off, from kerosene gas-powered Tilley lamps imported from the UK. Water was kept in receptacles and we did our best to keep insect larvae out of them. We simply drank the water and hoped for the best. Illnesses such as tapeworm, boils, and all types of fevers were common. Medication for fevers was often a pink coloured quinine tablet that could only be obtained from the post office. It was sent to Nigeria by the colonial administration in London.

By the time my other brothers and sisters were born, father instituted a regime of clean stomachs for the whole family because he believed that all illnesses came from having unclean bowels, like in Victorian England. And so, once every three months, the whole family took purgatives *en masse*, in order to rid us of illnesses, including worms. The diuretic was a foul smelling castor oil or *mist alba*. Another foul-tasting pill, *cascara sagrada* had an unbelievably foul smell especially when you started secreting it out. The whole smelly brew was relieved with a slice of sweet orange to clean the mouth after swallowing. The rest of the day, we just hung around and waited for our turn to run to the toilet. As the children and family of the house-owner, we had our own toilet separated from the communal one used by the tenants. It was a special room at the back of the house, next to the communal bathroom. You climbed a wooden box on which you squatted. There was a big hole in the middle of the wooden box. Under the hole was a pail where human excrement piled up. This was emptied every night at around 9 p.m. by a special team of people called night-soil men, instituted by the British administration. People who cleared night soil were extremely useful to the community because each time they went on strike for better pay and conditions, the whole city was paralysed.

You could not go to the toilet if your bucket was full. If this happened during the rainy season, my mother usually led a team of young men to carry the excretion out of the toilet and throw it into the raging torrents streaming past our back yard. You felt very clean when the rains came because the whole compound would have been swept clean and washed during the major rains, usually in July and August. Contrary to now, the rains were cold and many a child caught the chill because they had stayed too long under rainwater that cascaded from the roofs of our houses. And if you caught a cold, you had *mentholatum*, basically petroleum jelly laced with strong smelling oil of wintergreen, rubbed all over your chest. We always slept soundly during the rainy season because temperatures dropped to 20°C or less at night, from the 30°C we were used to. These were low temperatures with little or no humidity. Waking up in the morning was difficult and having a bath in the morning was a problem; you needed warm water to bathe. These mornings were cold during the rainy season. Papa, the patriarch, had water boiled for him and was informed when his bath water was ready. This was usually in a huge bucket of water. Soap and sponge were put on a dish next to that and his towel draped over the door of the bathroom. If there was any contagious illness in the neighbourhood, like chicken pox, father instituted a regime in which everybody in his immediate family had carbolic acid added to their bath water, as disinfectant.

At our home at 86 Clifford Road, we had a HMV (His Master's Voice) gramophone and records. To operate, the gramophone had to be physically wound up and needles changed every so often to get some sound out of the vinyl 78 rpm records. Our favourite tunes were Portuguese rumba. Father liked to play records on Friday nights.

On such nights, the Tilley lamp would be brought out and would provide lighting to within about 100 metres of our house. All the local kids would congregate in front of our house to listen to the records. Bedtime was about 11 p.m. when father would simply shut shop by stopping his gramophone. Kids had five minutes to run home before the lamp was switched off. In return for father's generosity, I had to polish his leather shoes and thigh-high leather boots every Sunday, whether he had worn them or not.

Our other major source of amusement as kids in Aba was going to the local cinema at Rex cinema at the Motor Park. As we lived at the bottom end of town, we would have to cross the principal market to get to the other part of town where the cinema was. I think Father did this trip twice in my lifetime – taking the whole family to the cinema. It was a major logistical nightmare because we would go as a group of at least five people, Papa, Mama, myself – their only child at this time – and two cousins who accompanied us for security. We carried a big torchlight because there were no street lamps. I do not remember being afraid of being attacked by robbers. Instead, the fear was of being attacked by mad people who passed the night at the central market place at Ehi Road. That was their only home. So going through the market at 8 p.m. on the way to cinema was absolutely terrifying. Films started at 9 p.m. and ended at about 11 p.m.

The return home from the cinema after 11 p.m. was also harrowing. In order to avoid the madmen in the market place at midnight, we took the longer route home, using only the major roads and avoiding the market altogether. Several years later, George Spiropoulos would come from his house at the upper end of town to convince my father to let me accompany him to the cinema. He saw me back to our place and then walked home with another friend to his house. What a fellow!

It was around 1947–1948 that our school, Christ the King School, Aba, put on the play *Robin Hood* and I was cast in the part of *Alan a Dale*. The play was so well received by the senior school (Standard 4 and 5), that we were asked to put it on for the local boy scouts who were on retreat in Aba and had camped on the grounds of St Michael's school, the Anglican Church school in Aba. I went to St Michael's to assist in the play and had not told either of my parents. At about 6.30 p.m. we finished our presentation and it was dusk. In the tropics, once the sun disappears it grows dark within thirty minutes. I set off for home in Clifford Road from St Michael's. I would not get home until after 7 p.m. By then it was really pitch-black and my parents would be worried. The fear in those days was that kids were kidnapped and sold into slavery or used for human sacrifice. My parents and relations were already out in the streets and had been looking for me for the best part of thirty minutes. I had never before come back late to the house and naturally my parents were terrified. I walked back oblivious of my parents' worries. When I got into our house, there was a deadly silence. My mother told me how worried they had been. My father sat on the veranda in a sort of rocking chair and did not utter a word.

As I sat down to explain where I had been, he grabbed me and gave me six lashes on my buttocks. I sobbed like mad. I think it was the thought that I had let my parents down rather than the pain that made me sob. That was one of the two times in my life that my father ever whipped me.

The second whipping offence was the day I went to a fast-moving river called Over Bridge on the edge of town, again with Georgie and other friends, to swim. This was a clean fast-flowing river at the other end of town on the way to Ikot-Ekpene. I can still today remember the sensation of jumping into the water, head first, with water going up my nose as I dived from the road bridge above. I remember diving deep into the water and simply hoping I would rise again. I was not a good swimmer but above all I knew I should not be there. I actually enjoyed the sensation, more like being intoxicated! My eyes were wide open under water and I could feel myself going deeper and deeper into the water without knowing if I could get up again. I did come up again, but short of breath.

On our way back we tied little knots in elephant grasses to put a spell on our parents so that they would not suspect we had been to the river. Every year, two or three people drowned in this fast-moving river and I was forbidden, as an only child, to go to that river, let alone swim in it. The elephant grass trick did not work and when we got back, a bit late and with my eyeballs red from diving into water, my father asked if I had been near the river. I could not say no. I got a good six lashes again and I cried. That was the last time Papa laid hands on me.

I went back to this river in June 2000 and was pleased to note it was still there, not as glorious as it was before, but still there. There is now a new and larger bridge over it. Unfortunately, huge parts of the river are obscured by rubbish that has accumulated over the years. At the far end of the bridge, at the old European quarter where English administrators swam and anchored their motorboats, a beer factory has been constructed, with two enormous effluent outlets directly plunged into the river. Effluents rich in phosphates are directly emptied into the river, resulting in very thick vegetation that has nearly choked off the river. Fortunately, there is a local environmental group protesting this abomination.

There were years we did not return to the village for the Christmas holiday season. We stayed in Aba and Papa would start getting ready for Christmas as early as November. This would be the beginning of the *Harmattan*, the cold dry wind from the north.

Mornings were characterised by real coldness and everyone would wear a second-hand sweater, an army grey-green leftover from the war. Mother would boil water to give me a wash before sending me off to school. Papa had a huge bucket of boiled water to which he added carbolic to give it a milky colour with a strong disinfectant smell.

In November, if it was going to be a good Christmas, Papa would buy a goat from the other part of town and have it delivered, live, to our house. It was now the job of one of my father's assistants and us kids to keep this poor tethered animal supplied with fresh grass every day, to give it water and generally look after it because we knew it would be part of our Christmas meal that year.

As Christmas drew near, all the children were excited and nervous about whether their parents would get them any presents. Top of the list of presents were new shoes and clothes. I was extremely privileged because I remember clearly as a nine- or ten-year-old receiving for Christmas an alpaca shirt (very itchy and expensive) and a pair of children's brown brogue shoes with crepe soles and a grey pair of socks.

In later years this was cause for lots of tears because I outgrew those beautiful brogue shoes and could not bear to lose them. They were simply perfect and I was like a little district officer. You received your presents on the day before Christmas (24th of December), so that you could wear them to mass on Christmas day to show off. So, you can imagine all these excited kids in new clothes trooping off to mass the next day, to show off their new presents!

At the age of nine, I was old enough to go to midnight mass with both my father and mother. It was pure magic. On other Christmas occasions, I went to the day mass with my mother. Papa stayed at home, either because he had already been to midnight mass, or as later in his life, he did not see why he should go to church to worship God. While we were at mass the goat would be slaughtered, to spare the young ones watching the poor animal put to death. I did watch the slaughter of a cow once and I was terrified as the animal screamed. By the time we returned from mass, usually after midday, we would be starving. We would see huge carcasses of goat meat ready for roasting on an open fire. Because it was Harmattan it would still be cold in the morning and on returning from mass, we would join in roasting the meat on the open fire at the back of our house.

Mother would probably have two or three other women helping her to cook a gigantic pot of rice, grind several kilograms of onions on open stone and cut up several kilograms of tomatoes, seasonings, etc. and bring all that together in a huge black pot. She would be cooking the sauce, into which huge pieces of goat meat would be thrown, to make a stew. The cooking was on huge open fires in the back enclosure of our house. There would be two or three cooking stalls, each attended by a young lady. Mama supervised. Every tenant in the house would come out to watch. One could smell this gorgeous feast from several metres away.

Come two o'clock, a steady stream of relations, acquaintances, friends and people unknown to us would arrive at our house, make a polite tap on a wide-open door and ask if there was anybody at home. I would receive them and ask them to sit down while I ran to the back of the house to scream for Mama or Papa, depending on the sex of the visitor. Papa or Mama would usually take over, offering the males a traditional welcoming gift of kola nuts and black pepper, a bit like the black pepper found in Europe. Rumour has it that people have killed their enemies by offering them kola nuts that were laced with poison. We were advised early in childhood never to eat kola nuts outside our house. For close friends, father would graduate from kola nuts to glasses of specially brewed palm wine. For his super friends, he would bring out his hidden green bottle of Schiedam aromatic schnapps imported from Holland. To a very special few, he offered his special bottle of Portuguese cognac smuggled from the Portuguese colony of Fernando Po, in Equatorial Guinea. It was an offence in British Nigeria of the 1940s to buy Portuguese or Japanese goods.

Japanese goods were already very good value at the time but were labelled *Fabrique en Japan* which was tantamount to second-hand. Today, Japanese watches are among the best in the world.

Portuguese brandy was relatively cheap and good enough for my father. He bought it on the black market from traders who visited us from Bamenda and Victoria, in the Cameroon. My father had a thriving business in rubber sheets, which he imported from the United Kingdom and sold in Aba to traders from Calabar and Cameroon. Papa was fluent in Efik, the language of the Calabar people, many of whom were his friends. Calabar women were reputedly the most beautiful in Nigeria, and keep their men by turning themselves into beautiful mermaids.

If the visitor to our house at Christmas was a close friend and came with his wife and children, the wife and children would be taken away from the visitor's parlour where my father held court. The wife and children went to my mother's room. There, they ate as much rice and meat as they could handle. Soft drinks like Coca-Cola were not around in Aba in the 1940s, and so women were offered a weaker version of palm wine called *ngwo* that was sweet, as against *nkwu* which was acidic, very concentrated and preferred by men. Christmas Day was thus a day of excessive eating and drinking, but come 4 p.m. when the sun was no longer too hot, troupes of dancers who had been practising their dance all year would suddenly appear before our door. The dancers would be dressed in very colourful costumes; there would be a band with various local Igbo instruments – flutes, drums, and xylophones, not unlike a Brazilian carnival.

They would arrive at our house, perform their stuff and, of course, you would hear them and Papa would go out and give them money for their sweat (a shilling or six pence for instance), or feed them. As soon as they left another group would turn up, and by sunset you could have had up to six troupes performing for our home and singing Papa's praise. It was great and we felt important. The end of Christmas Day was always an anti-climax and often sad.

All we had left was celebrating New Year's Day. New Year's Eve, December 31, in the 1940s, was right at the peak of the Harmattan season. Everything was dry. Our lips cracked from the dry wind and in some years it was bitterly cold. To stop our lips cracking, we rubbed lots of Vaseline on them. The weather in Aba is no longer like that nowadays. On New Year's Eve, according to Igbo traditions, all households had to throw out all their old household utensils. This was to say goodbye to the old year and to welcome the new one. But you could only do so at the stroke of midnight. That is when the Harmattan wind *ihu uguru* carries away with it the evils of the passing year. And so, at midnight, people lit up huge fires in the middle of the street, burnt old furniture and threw out old earthenware pots together with their rubbish and symbolically swept out their compounds of old habits and old spirits. The effect of this was that our street in Aba, Clifford Road, was littered with rubbish. The municipal council did the cleaning up two to three days later. They had to celebrate their own New Year's Day as well. For us kids it was fantastic, because we were allowed to stay up until midnight to watch what was happening from the security of the frontage of our house. There was all this light instead of the usual pitch-darkness of an African night.

But we also made our own fire works and explosives by ourselves. It was quite simple. We bought bits of calcium carbide from the market place. Calcium carbide was common in those days because it was used in some street lamps at the European end of town. Europeans burned acetylene generated from calcium carbide, and so calcium carbide was readily available. We took bits of calcium carbide and placed them inside the metal cover of a metal cigarette box (a Capstan cigarette cup was the best). We would spit on the calcium carbide causing it to fizz. By covering the fizzing solid/spittle mixture quickly with the other and larger half of the metal cigarette can, we collected a substantial quantity of acetylene gas. We had already drilled a hole in the larger half of the cigarette can. We would then place a lighted piece of stick at the perforated hole of the metal can. This would shoot into the air with an enormous bang. What we were doing without knowing it was generating acetylene, a highly inflammable gas, in a closed environment, the inverted cigarette tin. The only escape for this gas was the tiny hole at the top of the tin. A burning stick would thus ignite the enclosed gas in the cigarette tin, setting off an explosion. Papa forbade my friends and I from messing around with this contraption near our house. Some children had been injured when the explosion did not go up cleanly into the air and had hit their faces. More serious was the fact that all the houses in our neighbourhood were roofed with raffia. In the dry season, these roofs were as dry as tinderboxes. Stories every year told of houses set on fire by exploding cigarette cans!

Another exceptional event in the days of my childhood and growing up in Aba was changing the raffia roofing of houses. It was done as a co-operative because the work was too much for a household and nobody had enough money to pay professional roof-thatchers. Papa would warn us the week before that the roof would be changed on a given Saturday, and all through the preceding week, workmen would deposit layers and layers of raffia roofing in front of our house. On the appointed day, a minimum of fifteen men, usually relations and friends, would assemble at our house at about 6.00 a.m. Daybreak was never before 6 a.m., and when it arrived it was sudden and quick. The smaller children and myself would be awakened, half asleep, and taken out into the compound. A few of the men would climb the roofs and start cutting up the roofing and sliding it down. By 8 a.m., my bedroom, my father's, our whole house would be entirely without cover. After stripping the roof, the men would come down and be given breakfast by my mother. This was usually made up of *akara* (fried bean balls), maize porridge, and some dried fish if they were lucky, and palm wine.

Roof thatchers were the tough guys. They would climb back up at about 9 a.m., the sun gradually creeping up to the horizon. They sweated profusely. They were not afraid of heights and knew how to manoeuvre between the roof supports without breaking them or falling off. By about 2 p.m. when the sun would be at its zenith, they would finish the roofing and come down to well-deserved huge meals of pounded yam or cassava, meat and fish stew, washed down with palm wine.

The small ones like myself, accompanied by my mama, would be allowed back when it was all finished to gaze at the delicately thatched roofs, resplendent in green and the smell of fresh raffia. At night, we had a splendid fireworks display of burning old raffia at which we all assisted. Each time this rejuvenation of our roof occurred, I slept beautifully the next night. Why? Because the entire population of small beasts that had been living in the roof for the past two or three years (centipedes, millipedes, mice, cockroaches, etc.) had either been killed or run away. From then

on I could sleep for a few months without fear of hearing
something rustling in the roof! As kids, we were terrified of
centipedes or wall geckos dropping from the ceiling. Many years
later and even when I was in Europe as a student, I had a recur-
ring dream when I was uneasy about something. This dream
always consisted of arriving at our house at 86 Clifford Road and
finding the raffia roof leaking, and being very angry that the roof
had been allowed by the occupants and tenants of our house to go
into disrepair!

Going 'Home' to Akokwa

For town kids like myself, the biggest event of the year was going 'home' to the town or village of birth of our parents at Christmas time. For me, home was and still is Akokwa, the village from which both my parents came. We planned for this for weeks in advance, by buying new clothes, soap, dried tobacco leaves, beer and biscuits. These were articles from the big city for distribution to our village folk we would be visiting. After all, we were city folk! The journey was usually in a huge lorry converted into a sort of bus for conveying people. There weren't any buses then. There would be about 60 people, men, women and children in one of these lorries and it would leave Aba at about 8 a.m. to get to Akokwa, 120 km away, by 4 p.m., an average speed of 15 km per hour. This was because roads in Eastern Nigeria were not paved and half were washed away by heavy rainfall. The lorries we travelled in were old Bedford or Dodge lorries that had arrived in Aba as second-hand lorries from Lagos. The biggest fear was crossing any of the various rivers on our way, such as the Imo River at Owerrinta or going up the hills near Akokwa. The rivers were fast flowing and the bridges over them were just wide enough to take one lorry at a time. If the driver made the slightest correction while on the bridge, the lorry ended up in the river. As a young child I regularly dreamt of successfully crossing the Imo River at Owerrinta.

The actual journeys seemed interminable. I vividly remember standing in the front compartment of the lorry beside my mother and father and watching the palm trees along the route go round and round and round and follow us home. Akokwa, our hometown in Orlu District of Owerri Province, is red land country that looked even redder in December during the dry season. Everything about Akokwa was different from Aba. For a start, people in Akokwa stared at us a lot more than we were used to in Aba. They were mostly farmers and according to legend, they were mysterious people involved in all sorts of things including witchcraft or *juju*. We, the kids from Aba, were told not to go anywhere with strangers in Akokwa. The climate on the other hand was superb, primarily because the village had a lot of trees, was not crowded, was very windy and consequently not humid. It was said that the air in Akokwa restored people's health if they had been ill. I think the main reason was the reduced tempo of life and a lot more space and trees. There was no electricity though. At Grandmother's house, lighting was from palm oil-soaked sticks that burnt all night. This gave off a rich aromatic smell that remained with me all my childhood years as the authentic smell of Akokwa.

Water had to be fetched from a river about one kilometre from our house. My Auntie Maggie, my mother's youngest sister, whom I adored, initiated me and took me to this magical spring water source. It is still there today. We fetched water in earthenware vessels and walked for another kilometre to get home to Grandmother's compound. As night fell and especially at full moon, the young men of the village would stage a wrestling competition.

I watched in awe. Young maidens, bare-breasted, would come out also at night, at full moon, to dance in groups. They were absolutely gorgeous against a cloudless moonlit night. We were sexually aroused and because we were underage, we could not do a thing about it. Besides, both father and mother were strong Catholics at this stage and any adolescent lustfulness was out of the question.

Staying overnight for one or two days at Grandmother's house was magic. Not just because as her grandson, she let me run wild and do whatever I liked. It was also because her life rhythm, her way of doing things was different. It was evident to me as a nine-year-old that I was already conscious of the more relaxed quality of rural life compared with the overcrowding and rush in the cities. Water had to be fetched from a river. Cooking oil was pressed from freshly roasted palm fruits. The red earth was so dry that each time you threw water out on it, the smell of burnt earth came back to greet your nostrils. All around Grandma's house was life. Little goats and chickens clucked around the cooking hearth to eat leftovers. Because everyone around you in the compound was a family relation of one type or another, you felt extra secure, as a child. Occasionally some elders would warn us to be careful about certain individuals who were thought to be involved in the abduction of children. The mode order was not to follow strangers.

My father had over the years built a small three-bedroom bungalow on his land in Umuokwara village. In his homestead in Akwu village, my father had lived in a small house with his parents and his sister. Uncles and aunts lived in nearby houses within the same compound. When my father's father died, he lived with his sister and mother in this small house under the tutelage of his uncle. When my father's mother died, my father became an orphan and was brought up by his auntie. In those circumstances he was given very little of the land that rightly should have been passed on to him. Thus he had no choice but to rely on his in-laws, my mother's parents. Luckily, Onyenakala, my mother's father, had plenty of land in the adjoining village of Umuokwara. Onyenakala gave a large piece of land in Umuok-wara, as dowry, to my father Gabriel Ibekwe when he married my mother, Njanma. On this land, my father built a small bungalow to house his family on our visits from Aba. Today, the seat of the Ibekwe family in Akokwa is on this land that was a wedding present to my father from my grandfather, Onyenakala. Onyena-kala stipulated that the land was to be passed on to the first male child of Gabriel Ibekwe and Theresa Njanma Ibekwe. That land has now been passed on to me on the death of my father and it is today our family's seat in Akokwa and in Nigeria. Both my parents and one of my father's wives are buried there.

Shortage of land is the bane of the Akokwa people and all Igbo people. Thus having your own land is extremely important. My father was no exception. Land deprivation in my father's early life was to play a vital role in his later life as he spent a lot of time and money buying up land in Akokwa. This must have been quite considerable, as we found out in his will after his death. It now seems certain that in his lifetime he hated not having enough land for himself and for his family and so he did all in his power to buy up as much land as he could afford. All my father's land has now been distributed to his children from his three marriages.

Leaving Home

By 1948, I was twelve and in the fifth year of primary school, or
Standard 5. It was time to leave Aba and think of secondary
schools. The most prestigious secondary school in the East at that
time was Government College, Umuahia. My headmaster
suggested I took the entrance examination in 1948, a year ahead of
my school leaving year. The examination was carried out in the
premises of Government School, at School Road, Aba. Local
school headmasters supervised the examination. I failed and was
not offered a place at Government College, Umuahia. One of my
friends, Henry Obineche, passed. I was badly shaken. That was
my first-ever external examination. The school headmaster, John
Edemanya, was certain I could do better and that perhaps I had
panicked at the examinations. He persuaded my father to enrol
me in an after-classes study group. The teacher was a young man,
a cousin of the headmaster. He was great and because he was only
in his twenties, we could talk to him and not be afraid. I worked
hard at my arithmetic and geography, my weak subjects at the
time. There were eight of us kids and classes were held in the
teacher's house. In addition to studies, I had my first puff of a
cigarette in this teacher's house. We rolled our own cigarettes
from bits of tobacco left in empty cigarette cans. We collected the
tobacco and, instructed by an older boy, wrapped them in bits of
paper and smoked them. We all choked and coughed violently at
our first cigarette and all had dizzy spells.

Mama sold cloth and ladies' dresses. She was a good seam-
stress and taught me how to sew, thread needles and sew buttons,
activities that helped me later as a bachelor. As early as 7 a.m. I
would be at my mother's stall in the main market in Aba to
display my mother's newly sewn dresses for sale. After displaying
her goods, I would ask a neighbour to look after them until my
mother would arrive at about 7.30 a.m. There was no question of
any goods being stolen. If it happened, it would have to be a

'foreigner', somebody from out of town. That person would probably be killed by the market mob, infuriated at such disgraceful happening. At home, I had progressively become more religious and went through a phase in which everything the priest said at mass was true and had to be strictly adhered to. At this stage I was a regular attendant at morning mass, nearly every day of the week. This was a difficult, but at the same time, exhilarating experience. My mother would wake me up at 5.30 a.m. and I would wash my face. She and I would then proceed, with me half-asleep, through the morning mist to the church compound. Mass would start at 6.00 a.m. and end at about 6.30 a.m., enough time to come back home, have breakfast and then proceed to install my mother's goods at her post in the market.

Meanwhile, my religious fervour had not gone unnoticed and attracted two bizarre and very different reactions. On one hand, a parish priest from Christ the King Church visited our home and spoke to my parents about the parish priest's belief that I might have a calling for the priesthood. My mother, who was always a strong believer, was delighted and said, why not? My father, always a pragmatist, said I was too young and that they should come back in two years time to see how I felt. I myself had no strong feelings one way or another, other than to see miracles or pray that Christ revealed his wishes to me.

At the other end of the scale, my best friend George Spiropoulos told all our friends that I had gone pious and that each time I entered the Catholic mission compound, I would not speak because I considered it a sin to talk or gossip in the House of God. I had for some reason or the other taken literally the need to respect church premises, especially when the *Sacristi* was exposed, to mean the whole of church premises. I actually felt that ordinary people were not so respectful on church grounds and this had to be checked by example! And so for the best part of a year, my friends made my life hell. Each time they saw me in the mission premises they would start teasing me to make me react and talk. I actually held my ground and did not talk. That was my first experience of holding my ground. It was tough but I succeeded.

One pleasant and unexpected result of this religious fervour was to come in the dreams I had in those days. For years as a young child, I very often ended my dreams each night by a trip into the jungle where we would see all sorts of wonders and animals. Near my waking up time, there would always be a terrifying beast, a lion or, more often, a snake chasing us. I always had great difficulties running away and escaping. I later discovered by myself, as a ten-year-old, that I always fell in my dreams, or had difficulty running fast away from the chasing beast because I slept in a coiled position, foetus position, with my legs coiled up under me. I never again slept in a coiled position after that discovery. From that day on, my legs were fully stretched when I slept and, interestingly enough, I ran like a gazelle when I was chased in the dark forests of my dream. An added bonus from this religiousness was also that I had angels who assisted me when I was in trouble.

In particular, if I had a frightening dream, which for many children would result in a nightmare and in screaming, I would always have the same fantastic escape route. When chased in the jungle, after running for a while, I would kick my heels together and immediately this would propel me into the air and I would start flying. I would not have wings, but I would be super light and would glide in the air between trees and houses and way above the city houses. To land, I would follow a light beacon, like an aeroplane coming in to land and locked on to radar. My 'radar' was a beam of light that I would follow in the jungle as I was chased by beasts and between houses. Safe landing was me flying and following this guiding light between houses and trees and landing safely on my bed in our house at 86 Clifford Road, Aba. At that instant, my eyes would open and I would awaken in my bedroom, feeling safe. The guiding light I followed in my flight was no other than a small egg-shaped lamp that was always alight all night in my bedroom as a child. I do not know why my mother did that, but it was clear later in my life that this was what I needed. I was probably afraid of the dark as a child. Many years later, as an adult living in Europe, I still had dreams in which I floated and flew over buildings. So strong were these feelings that I found myself once in a semi-sleepy condition in the morning, wondering if I had not just been flying! Being religious can be fantastic for your imagination! And just as I tried to cope with my religiousness, sex also began to rear its head. There were two enormous temptations – one was Victoria or Vicky – George Spiropoulous' sister. With a Greek father and Nigerian mother, Vicky was one of the most beautiful girls I had ever seen. I think we all adored her. Vicky was older than Charlie, who was older than George, who was a year older than I was.

In 1948, Vicky was at least five years older than our age group. But Vicky was often with her two brothers and we all played together in the tall grasses at the back of St Joseph's College, the girls' teacher training college in Aba. We did not get up to anything naughty, but our senses were aroused and I felt quite sinful just thinking about her. I believe I confessed to having 'dirty thoughts' to Father Hampson or Stiegler at the confessional. My other problem was the daughter of a pharmacist, Mr Wadibia, the owner of the Emy cinema, Aba. I do not remember her name now. Her father was a well-educated Rivers (Mbammili) man who was a cut above the local traders. The girl, as I vaguely remember, was rather attractive with soft gentle features that came from good breeding. She was also more of my age group, but attended Government School, Aba. I was at Christ the King School, Aba, and so I could only see her after school when I would visit my father's shop at 33 Asa Road, Aba. I was a bit crazy about her. The family lived not very far away in Hospital Road, but the children always hung around the cinema in Hundred Foot Road that was next door to my father's shop. Her brother was also my friend but did not exactly promote our association. Nothing came of the relationship, especially since I was to proceed to King's College, Lagos, soon after. All in all, I was an innocent romantic. I cannot say that for Georgie who was altogether much more knowledgeable about these things. The girls simply adored Georgie.

Papa was by now very busy with the Aba town council. The Resident of Owerri Province, the highest-ranking British Administrator in Eastern Nigeria came to Aba and took pictures with the council members. Other big wigs including Commissioners etc visited, and told them what His Majesty's government expected of them. There was order, very little crime and a sense of going somewhere. Our mud-walled house was rebuilt into a concrete building with corrugated iron roofing. The construction started with the front part of the building and we lived in the tenants' quarters behind. When the front was completed, we moved into it and the remainder of the building was completed, around 1949. Just around the same time, Papa bought a second-hand ex-army truck which he and Michael, an ex-soldier and a cousin on my mother's side, converted into a type of bus for carrying passengers from Aba to Akokwa. It was the first ever direct transport from Aba to Akokwa, and it was named 'One with God is a Majority'. Before it, we used trucks going to Arondi-zuogu, a neighbouring village, and it took all day. Michael was the driver and he made sure he returned every day from his trip to Akokwa. I would hear them discussing the day's account, how many passengers, petrol cost, etc. Michael gave me three pence to hire bicycles to ride. I had learnt how to ride three years earlier.

At about this time, Papa was also beginning to feel successful. His friends in Aba included a number of prosperous traders, like Remy Okoro of Arondizuogu and Okoro's cousin who was chairman of Aba Urban District Council. Vincent Okoro, Remy's son, was a friend and a contemporary. If you felt you were doing well, you showed this by buying a car or marrying a second or third wife. In 1948, my father married a second wife, Rosalind, in accordance with Nigerian customary law. Rosa, as we called her, was nice and soon fitted into the household.

Emma, my younger brother was born soon afterwards and we became a very close family unit again. At last Mama had a second child in eleven years, after all the deaths of my earlier brothers and sister. As a result of this second marriage, my father was now in a polygamous marriage. The Catholic Church frowned on polygamy and he could no longer go to mass as he used to do, or receive Holy Communion.

From then on, Mama would put on her best clothes on Sunday; dress Emma and myself up and take us to the Christ the King Church in Aba on her own. This was the key event of the week. Papa would stay at home and clean the barrels of his shotgun. Something had changed. It was as if a certain innocence and carefree life had disappeared. Polygamy was clearly in vogue in Igbo land at this time, and having more than one wife showed you were rich. In any case, there was a serious demographic imbalance in Igbo land at this time. There were many more females than males. Male children appeared to be less resistant to the illnesses that prevailed and so male infant mortality was particularly high. The result was a shortage of males to marry the girls back home in the villages. The only way out was polygamy. It was economically ruinous and could not have made sense to the money-conscious Igbo man. There had to be another reason – prestige. You were more like a chief if you had more than one wife. Following this logic, Papa would marry his third wife, Laeticia, some years later. This was nothing when compared with the seven wives of my uncle, my father's brother. We did get on very well with my half brothers and sisters as they grew up. However, our father's finances were stretched to the limit in trying to feed and clothe the new additions to his family. The social cost of polygamy is visible everywhere in Nigeria.

By the end of 1948 I wanted to leave home. I was twelve. Mama was unhappy because our resources were insufficient to feed our enlarged family. For the first time in my life I heard Mama arguing with father about provisions made for us. In this new atmosphere, Mama was to give birth to three other children after Emmanuel. So in effect, even if they had arguments and there were two other women in the household, Papa slipped out some nights to go to Mama's room where they made babies. As a twelve-year old, I did not know how they did it without waking up the others! Whatever the case was, it was time for me to leave home and in the summer of 1948 I sat for a raft of entrance examinations to various secondary schools including: St Patrick's College, Ikot-Ansa, Calabar; St Patrick's College, Asaba; and King's College, Lagos.

My result of the year earlier haunted me. I had failed the entrance examination to the prestigious Government College at Umuahia. Perhaps I was too young to sit for that examination at the age of eleven. This time I passed the entrance examinations to St Patrick's Ikot-Ansa, St Patrick's Asaba and King's College, Lagos. The results to St Patrick's Ikot-Ansa and Asaba came early in 1949 and so I proceeded to both Ikot-Ansa and Asaba for interviews. I was leaving home for the first time and I was terrified. In addition, mosquitoes literally ate us alive at the boarding houses we were placed in. I was depressed, but still happy I could go to college. One of my friends, Henry, had passed to Government College, Umuahia. Georgie also was off to Christ the King College at Onitsha. The truth was that neither Umuahia, Ikot-Ansa nor Asaba appealed to me – they lacked the vibrancy of Aba.

I would be going into the bush if I went to any of these colleges. A few months later, in July 1949, a miracle happened. My father received a government telegram telling him that I had passed the entrance examination to King's College, Lagos, the Nigerian Eton! Joy was mixed with trepidation. Could we afford it? Everything was turned upside down. There was only one other boy from Aba who had got into King's college – Benjamin 'Mersh' Maduka. We were to be the toast of Aba Township. We were the first and supposedly the cleverest kids Aba had ever produced. Only one other kid ever got to King's College again from Aba – and that was Augustine Ibegbulam who ended up as principal of King's College in the 1980s.

I now had to go to Lagos, the capital, for the interview. The British founded King's College, Lagos, in 1905, for the children of colonial civil servants and the children of the Nigerian elite. I had never left Eastern Nigeria before and the journey to Lagos took four days (three nights). Who would look after me in Lagos? Fortunately, we had a countryman, a man from our village called Emmanuel Abalam who was a junior officer in the Nigerian police force and was at that time living in Obalende police barracks, Lagos. Father got word to him through traders who travelled to Lagos from Onitsha. He was to look after me as guardian during my stay in Lagos for this crucial interview for entry into King's College. I travelled to Lagos by train from Aba railway station in September 1949 on government warrant, with Benjamin Maduka. My mother had prepared enough food to last me for the three nights the journey would take. Poor Mama was terrified and very distressed and she broke down in tears as the train pulled away. Who could blame her? For the last eleven years, I was the only child, three others children having died from illness.

Of course Emma and John were already born and kept Mama busy. But Emma was only a toddler and John was not even a year old. The train that had arrived from Port Harcourt left Aba railway station at about 10 a.m. There was an Igbo trader who lived in Northern Nigeria who was in the same train compartment as myself. My parents naively asked him to look after me. In those days, there was no reason to think this fellow would do otherwise. But supposing he had kidnapped me and gone on to sell me in the North into slavery? Benjamin and myself did not worry about that and it did not cross our minds. I was grateful an Igbo was on the train.

Our steam train filled with water, blew its whistle and then steamed off. Averaging about 35 miles per hour, we steamed through the lush green forests of Aba/Umuahia with villages of small-corrugated houses surrounded by rows and rows of yam plants on sticks, on to the red and relatively arid plains of the Savannah near Enugu. We were at least still in Igbo land and understood the language. We reached Enugu by late evening, at about 6 p.m., having covered a distance of 150 miles in about eight hours, with frequent stops in between. Benji and I did not say much to each other. We were busy looking at all the things around us. Starting from tonight, we would be out of Igbo land, meeting different types of Nigerians, people who looked different, spoke differently and even ate different food. We would be going into the north, the land of the Tivs, the Hausas and the Fulanis. These were predominantly Moslems or animists, with carefully coded behaviour patterns between the chiefs, bosses and others. People respected titles and kept to their places. We called them *Ranka Dede*. I had just come from Igbo land which was 80% Christian – mostly Catholic and temperamentally republican in outlook.

We had chiefs in Igbo land, but that was no big deal. The chief was only a title-holder, but the chief cannot tell anyone, especially people like my father who was an elected president of our local town union, what to do. The riots in Aba in 1929 had made it clear that the Igbos did not believe in chiefs. In effect, I was going to another world which would change my life forever.

The Nigerian railway system consists of 4,312 kilometres of single track and 1.06 metre wide rail gauge. There are two main lines starting from Port Harcourt in the East and from Lagos, the capital, in the west. The two lines run north and merge at Kaduna. From Kaduna, one line goes on through Zaria to Kano and then to Nguru in the northeast. The other line runs to Gusau and Kaura Namoda in the northwest, near the border with Niger Republic. By the time we left Enugu, it was pitch-dark as we hurtled through the night. Morning on the second day would break on a stony, semi-arid land with stunted trees and grassland. We were on the edge of the middle belt of Nigeria. By midday we reached Markurdi and crossed the River Benue. Here the train would stop and gorgeous portions of fried fish from the Benue river were on offer. I could not afford to buy any. Besides, I had my meals already prepared by my mama in my Jerry can. I would open various compartments of my Jerry can and find a scene of utter desolation! Moulds were beginning to grow on my boiled rice, my chicken stew and meat stew. With hindsight, this was not surprising since all that food was left in a closed, hot and humid compartment for twenty-four hours. This was to be a useful lesson in years to come, for Mama learnt how to cook stew in oil, without water in order to get it to last longer.

The people who sold fish, oranges, bush meat etc., were nice and polite, generally tall and darker than people I had known in the East. We had been warned not to mess around with them because most of them carried daggers for their protection. The train journey by now was monotonous, tedious and seemed to go on forever. Harsh granite rocks would reflect the blazing sun as our train passed. We were now in the plateau region of Nigeria. The vegetation did not change for the whole day, and by the end of the second day with the train getting near to Kafanchan in the real North of Nigeria, we were filled with excitement and fear. Kafanchan was the last major stop before we got to the big intersection in Kaduna where all the wagons were shunted around to head for Lagos, Kaura Namoda, Nguru or Port Harcourt. You dared not board the wrong train because you would end up in a part of Nigeria you had never heard of.

By the time the train stopped in Kaduna, it was nearly midnight on the second day. For me, a youngster of twelve, I really was in another country. People wore long dresses with skullcaps

(Muslim dress). Women were entirely covered by clothing. The air we breathed was drier and thinner and there was a strong smell of perfume, even at the railway station. There were lots of oranges, bread and sugar cane for sale, but not what we called real food in the East, like goat meat, chicken and yams. By and large, we found nobody who spoke Igbo or English and that completed my sense of alienation. To cap it all, it was really cold at night. A few brave souls stepped out of the train compartment to stretch their legs and get some fresh air. I was terrified to lose my place near the window in our coach. Worse still, I could miss our coach and get on a wrong coach and be shunted onto a train heading for the far north-eastern city of Maiduguri on the edge of Lake Chad.

By the early hours of the morning of the third day our train pulled off, heading southwest for Lagos and the homeland of the Yorubas. At least, so we hoped. We were now in the third day of the journey and had completed half the trip. We were heading south again. We were dirty, not having had any fresh water for two days. The drinking water we had in our glass bottles could not be spared for washing. The afternoon was very hot and the landscape was even more bare and unpopulated than what we had seen the day before. We were now heading for Jebba on the River Niger, the river that gave Nigeria its name. We would hurtle down semi-arid lands with nomadic people tending their cattle all along the railway line. Vast spaces of uninhabited land greeted our eyes. You must remember I had come from Aba, a bustling commercial town heavily populated with traders. Seeing such vast empty landscape was new and bewildering for me. The third day of the trip was without doubt the worst. I was running short of food supplies, and whatever was left in my Jerry can was now inedible from moulds growing on it. Clean drinking water was only possible if you could run down from the train when it stopped and fill your bottle from the big water gushers used for filling the train. The toilets in the train, mainly holes in the train floor emptying on to the rail tracks, were stinking and disgusting. You had to be really desperate to go into them on the third day. We were mostly exhausted and quiet as the train pushed on, slowly and continuously, up some small hills in the vicinity. Suddenly in late afternoon we approached the town of Jebba, which was agreeable enough. I was able to buy some fried fish and ate my fill. The train meandered past some difficult terrain and we approached the bridge of the majestic River Niger.

It was a beautiful sight as the train passed. I had never seen such a wide breadth of water in my life. Soon it would be dark, taking us into the fourth and final day of this incredible journey.

Morning would break on the final and fourth day to a much greener landscape with trees, and not the savannah and grass landscape of the past two days. We were now in Western Nigeria, in the land of the Yorubas. Some of the crops they grew were similar to ours in the East. The dresses people wore were however very different. They wore clothes that looked like jumpers with soft hats, unlike our clothes in the East. In the East, men tended to wear shorts or trousers or tied wrappers around their waists. Women wore blouses with wrappers below. In the North, the Moslems wore white dresses. What we saw in the West were multicoloured clothes with a predominance of a deep blue–indigo colour. Both men and women wore robes or *agbada*. As the train gathered speed we realised that we were now going down a sort of slope towards the sea. Names like Ilorin and Oshogbo that we had learnt in our geography classes suddenly came alive. The air was also less dry, more humid like in the East. I was very excited to be getting to my destination. We passed Ibadan and I knew we were no more than 120 kilometres from Lagos. By about 4 p.m. on the fourth day after I left Aba, we pulled into Iddo railway station in Lagos. It was fabulous. There were so many people and the station was large compared with our little station at Aba. I had finally arrived in Lagos, the capital of colonial Nigeria. Benji's family friends collected him. Emmanuel Abalam, the policeman from my village of Akokwa, was at the railway station for me.

We took a local red bus owned by J N Zarpas and Co, to go to Obalende Police Barracks. The homes were in rows, very much like the police barracks in Aba, but much larger, with a huge athletics field in the middle quadrangle. I spent the night there and the next morning I was taken to King's College in Lagos.

King's College was as beautiful and spectacular as I had thought it would be. It was situated opposite the largest race-course in the country. The main building is an old stone structure constructed in 1905 with classrooms, laboratories and the principal administrative building. This dominated the concourse. The rest of the buildings were newer and housed the halls of residence for the students. These houses were built around a concourse of athletics, football, hockey, cricket and squash fields. At the front of King's College was this magnificent race course which today has been ploughed in, to make way for a military parade ground! To the left were the Supreme Court and the Civil Service secretariat. To the right were the offices of the Lagos town council. The governor's residence at the marina was a stone's throw away. It was all very beautiful and very impressive for an Aba boy. Students in brilliant white shirts, shorts, trousers and brown sandals moved up and down staircases, changing classes. Everybody appeared to speak in English. The self-assuredness of these kids had to be seen to be believed. The older students stared at us new arrivals for interviews with an amused derision, as if to say they did not expect us to be accepted. There were very many of us, enough to field several football teams, and these interviews had gone on all week.

When our turn arrived, about 35 of us were moved into a classroom where we were once again given a written examination. I suppose this was the first chance for the school authorities to reassure themselves that the entrance examination results that brought us to the interviews had actually been done by us. The examination lasted about an hour and I cannot remember what it was about. I do however remember the oral examinations very well. Each of us twelve-year-olds was ushered into a room with two Englishmen and I think an African teacher as well. They asked questions in English to which we replied in English as well. I think I was nervous but not terrified, after all we had lived with and seen Europeans in Aba, and my local priests were French. We had a break after the oral examinations and were then offered lunch by the school. The decisive test would come later on that evening on the football pitch.

Apparently, I was literally in the last ten of the 60 boys accepted in September 1949 to start school in January of 1950. I was later told that I had played 'a blinder' at the outside-left position of the team I was in. The sports master, Mr Enyeazu, who, incidentally, was an Ngwa man from Aba, was very impressed and I think that sealed my fate. He actually told me not to worry and that I would be selected, and that he wanted me in the junior football team known as 'the mosquitoes'. Benji, my other mate from Aba, appeared to have sailed through easily. He was always precocious and even at that early stage already spoke English with a fancy posh accent. He was a natural for King's College. The day after the interview I boarded a train at Iddo railway station, Lagos, for the return journey to Aba. I do not recall much about the journey back to Aba, but it was another four gruelling days to Eastern Nigeria via Northern Nigeria.

This time I did not have my mama's cooking, and made do with whatever I could buy along the trip. The journey was not traumatic because we were on our way home and time went by very quickly. I was very elated on the fourth morning of the return trip, when I opened my eyes and realised we were on the outskirts of Enugu. The trees, the smells, the people – all looked familiar. I was back home in Igbo land. We got to Aba around midday to be greeted by my father, mother and small brothers.

I had been away for a great adventure in the capital and I had come back home. I was so happy, and so were my parents. We would have to wait for a further two months to know if I had been accepted by King's College. Time moved so slowly in those eight weeks and I did not do anything to advance my entry into either St Patrick's College, Calabar or St Patrick's Asaba, two institutions who had already offered me places. After what I had seen in Lagos, I had to wait for my chance at King's College, Lagos. That was the school for me!

For the next two months, my life was 'on hold'. I was listless and in a limbo, and not interested in doing anything. The examinations for the School Leaving Certificate (Standard 6) were due in about a month but I had no energy to prepare for them. All that mattered was how well I had done at my interview at King's College. Later that year we sat for our School Leaving Certificate and because of my experience of doing several entrance examinations, I 'walked' the Standard 6 School Leaving Certificate examinations. I was to get very good marks when the results were announced in December of 1949.

My friends like Henry Obineche who had passed to the prestigious Government College Umuahia, were now at this time buying their clothes and books to move to college. Georgie Spiropoulous was on his way to Christ the King College, Onitsha. Vincent Okoro went on to St Patrick's College, Calabar. Remarkably, the parents of all my friends wanted us all to go on to secondary education. None of our parents had been to secondary schools and they were convinced that the only way to get us away from being petty traders like themselves was to send us to secondary schools.

As will become apparent later on, they could not really afford the cost of secondary education. The average school fee for a border in a residential school was about £36.00 per year, or £3 per month. To see this in its true perspective, it must be remembered that my father usually gave about one shilling to my mother to prepare soup for six of us to last three days. £3 per month was equivalent to the salary of a senior government official. The so-called merchants or traders, like my father, probably made just a little bit more but they had so many dependants – in the village and in the city, to look after.

At the beginning of November 1949, a telegram arrived at our 86 Clifford Road, Aba residence. It was addressed to Mr G M Ibekwe, my father. I was still at school at Christ the King School preparing for my school-leaving certificate. My father, who by now was familiar with receiving government circulars as a member of Aba Urban City Council, read it. I shall never know how he reacted because I was not there.

It was from the principal of King's College, Lagos, Mr J R Bunting. It simply said 'Your son, Samuel Ibekwe, was successful at the interview in Lagos and had been offered a place for the year starting January 1950 at King's College, Lagos'. My father was required to answer yes or no by a given date if we wanted the place. On receipt of that reply, the school would send by post the cost of schooling at King's and what clothing would be needed for pupils like me who would be boarders. When I returned from school, my father handed me the telegram and I simply could not contain my joy! It was the first time in my young life that I had really gained something that I wanted so badly.

My parents were also very pleased. The word soon got out that I had gained admission to a school in the capital, Lagos. Nobody locally knew what to expect. We had to wait for the detailed letter from Lagos accepting me as a pupil and telling us what to do. The letter duly arrived and it was a bit of a shock. The list of clothing required ran to two pages and it was clear that procuring all that would be an enormous burden on my father.

Everything needed was to be provided, fourfold and in white – four white shirts, shorts, long trousers, jackets, pants, singlets, bed sheets, pillow cases, white canvas shoes and brown sandals. Sports shirts and shorts were in khaki. My father immediately contacted a local tailor and gave him the job of making all my clothes within two months from the cloth we had bought locally. I was the prince and everything would be subjugated in the next few months to getting me ready for Lagos.

As time went by, it became clear that my father could not afford to buy all the clothes and other things I needed for King's College and at the same time pay the tuition and boarding fee of £35 per annum. In addition to the school fees, he was required to make available to me twelve shillings of pocket money per term. My father contacted my uncle, Chief Mathias Okafor, in Onitsha and a few other members of our Umudieleke family group and each was asked to make some contribution towards paying my fees that, at the end of six years, would amount to over £250. That was a lot of money in 1949; it has to be remembered that a brand new Austin saloon car in those days probably cost about £200 pounds. My father despatched me to Onitsha to go and lobby for some of the money. What I remember was a lot of promises from all and sundry. There may have been some contribution, perhaps no more than a couple of pounds, to which my father added to pay the first term's fees, and after that my father had to bear the full burden alone. We certainly felt it because through my six years at King's College, I had to scrape to get by. My clothes were longer and larger than those of other kids were. That way, I grew into them and my parents did not have to make new ones when the old ones became too small. Across the other part of town, Benji Maduka's preparations ran smoothly, without a hitch. His father had a shop below their house at the junction of Asa Road by Ehi Road. They were relatively rich and prosperous. Benji already had several brothers and sisters older than himself and who had gone to secondary school. They, as a family, were more bourgeois and educated than my family.

I was the first child from my family to go to secondary school. In our home village of Akokwa, I was probably in the first ten people from that village to go to a secondary school. Either way, what was happening was a huge challenge and we could not afford to fail. My father had given all he could to make sure we seized advantage of this unique chance which passing the entrance examination to the prestigious King's College, Lagos offered. I do not remember much about the last days in Standard 6 and the 1949 School Leaving Certificate examinations. They really did not matter because I would be going to a new world and away from my contemporaries. It was very much like my first day at kindergarten, eight years ago – I was once again leaving my friends to enrol in a prestigious establishment, many miles away. There was a lot of unspoken pride but I suspect a lot of apprehension on all sides.

My mother in particular seemed to beam with pride each time our eyes met. But behind the pride and smile was the fear that I would probably be changed forever and that she would lose me in the process. And change I did, but my mother did not lose me! The Christmas and new year celebrations in 1949 seemed to rush by because all I was focused on was whether I had all my gear for going into King's College. In early January 1950, my warrant arrived from King's College. I was to exchange it for train tickets that would take me from Aba to Iddo Station, Lagos. I had made it and I was ready to fly!

A New Boy at King's College, Lagos

Train tickets were small cardboard pieces that had to be punched to validate them. I duly exchanged my warrant for tickets at the Aba railway station and waited for the great day when I would depart for my studies. The day arrived, somewhere in mid January 1950. On this momentous day, my mother had been up since 5.00 a.m. preparing chicken and beef stews and cooking them in pure palm oil with no water, to prevent them growing mouldy in the train. She had also boiled rice and yams and each of these items was put in a separate compartment in a Jerry can. Drinking water was stored in 75 centilitres old brandy bottles. Peeled oranges and bananas were wrapped in old newspapers. I took also with me some old army pullovers with holes in them for keeping warm during the long night hauls in Northern Nigeria. In addition to all this, my new white clothes and sheets were packed into two metal boxes that were to travel with me to Lagos. By about 8.00 a.m. my father, my mother, my two little brothers and a coterie of well-wishers took a local bus and rode on bicycles to get to the railway station in Aba, in the European section of town. Our first action on reaching the railway station was to go to the stationmaster and have my luggage registered for transportation in the luggage compartment of the train. You had to make sure it was done right otherwise you would arrive at your destination without your luggage. It was all very British. The railway station had all sorts of people waiting for the train – traders going back to the North with enormous loads of goods. Also present were Benjamin Maduka, his father, mother and sisters.

It was the big day out for the family. Unknown to us was the fact that Aba was also the gathering station for a number of other King's College students from Owerri Province. And also to our great surprise, a number of girls had turned up at the station to travel to Lagos. They also were going to the premier girls' college, Queen's College, Lagos. Both King's College boys and Queen's

College girls had the exclusive use of a coach which was designated for us. It was like a day out at Ascot. None of us kids knew each other. It was our first meeting. The only person I knew was my classmate, Benji Maduka. Needless to say, this was a much more agreeable scene than the first time I went to Lagos for that interview. This time there were a lot more kids of our age and secondly, we had a coach to ourselves, to the envy of every other passenger.

We looked different – the boys and girls going to King's and Queen's Colleges. We were all smartly dressed and as sharp as buttons! Somebody spotted the train from Port Harcourt and yelled that it was on the way to the station at Aba. Many years later, I would have many a pleasant dream in which the train from Port Harcourt featured. As the train pulled in to the platform, we all looked for the special wagon reserved for King's and Queen's Colleges. And by Jove it was there, clearly marked for all to see. There were already a few students in the coach – new students originating from the Rivers Province. We from Aba climbed into our coach, took up our seats and then went to the windows to look for our parents and relations. The scene on the platform was of panic and desolation. Parents were anxious that their children got into the right coach.

No sooner was that over than they realised that their best and brightest were going away to distant lands they would probably never visit. Worse still was the knowledge that we would not come back for vacation until July 1950, a good seven months away. That was devastating for any family, but especially so in Nigeria which was so vast and frankly hardly developed at the time. What would happen to us in Lagos? For us kids, our pain and panic was considerably lessened because we were so excited to be going to a new place, a new experience. The train finally pulled away from Aba railway station. We watched our parents, all in tears, as the train pulled off from the station. I stuck by the window and looked back at the station as my dear Aba and parents gradually disappeared in the distance and became only a tiny speck. The train was in full steam on the way to Umuahia, a mere 35 kilometres north. We were still in the black soil of Igbo land and so it was not so bad. The food crops on the farms we passed by were still familiar – yams, cassava, maize. Within the train coach, there were several young boys and girls in the twelve to thirteen age group. We made attempts to talk to each other but without much success because we were all more concerned about the future ahead of us. A few of us, including myself, were still in tears and missing our parents very much. The 'toughies' did not give a damn. The train pulled in at Umuahia railway station and now it was our turn to watch the new King's and Queen's College arrivals. Those of us who climbed on board in Port Harcourt and Aba had made sure we took the best seats in the coach, the window seats. The others would have to sit wherever they could. The kids who climbed on board at Umuahia were from the hinterland of Owerri Province. They were not to be compared with the Port Harcourt or Aba boys and girls because we had come from the cities.

They looked poorer than we did but we were all destined for King's and Queen's Colleges and that was what mattered. Our train left Umuahia for Enugu, the last major town in the East, the last city in Igbo land, before climbing into the hills of the North. We got to Enugu as the sun was beginning to dip into the horizon. It was about 6.00 p.m. King's and Queen's College students from the Igbo heartland of Onitsha Province – people from Awka, Onitsha, Umuoji and Enugu – joined the train in Enugu. Our coach was full by this time except for a few places left for students who might join us from the Middle Belt. I do not remember any students joining our train again after Enugu. There were not many students from the North in those days. Western Nigerian students at King's College were either already resident in Lagos and were thus day students or they came from cities like Ibadan, Abeokuta, etc., which were no more than about 120 kilometres from Lagos. They had a different transport arrange-ment from us students from the East. When our train pulled in at Enugu, we saw a railway station that was large and well planned. Enugu was known as the coal city. Nigeria's only coal mine was in Enugu and consequently there was a substantial expatriate English community in the city to run the mines. Enugu which means 'Top of a Hill' in Igbo is a rugged hilly town at the foot of a ridge of mountains which continues north to the Jos plateau in

Northern Nigeria. As a result, the climate is very agreeable, dry and cool. We got out of the train in Enugu to stretch our legs after the newcomers had taken their places in the coach. It was relatively familiar territory. People spoke Igbo and if they entered our coach by mistake we could talk to them in the local language and persuade them to go to other coaches because ours was reserved.

Later on, in Northern Nigeria, this would be impossible and we would have to ask railway guards to throw out a man carrying a dagger who wanted to sit in our compartment irrespective of the fact that it was clearly marked 'Reserved by order of Government.' This man did not see why we should be so privileged when he could not find seats in the other coaches. We were a bit hungry in Enugu and it was time to eat. Those of us who had brought food in our Jerry cans opened up and began to take out delicious legs of fried chicken and rice. Alas, some of the kids, especially those who came from rural communities, did not have much to eat. They had never seen a Jerry can before, let alone filled with food for a four-day journey. I shared a bit of my food with one or two kids who looked very hungry. After all, I had to make sure that I had enough food to last me for another three days. Enugu was the gathering point for Igbo students from Onitsha and Awka areas. The older King's College students who came on board looked arrogant, relaxed and sure of themselves. Once we had eaten and drunk some water (there was no Coca-Cola in those days), we were happy and ready to doze off. It was pitch dark by 7.00 p.m. and all good kids would be expected to sleep by then. That was not so easy. Here was a coach full of kids who looked relatively prosperous in a desperately poor country. If anybody decided to raid us, we would not be able to resist. So we shut the connecting doors between our coach and the other coaches and barricaded ourselves in. The older students took guard in turn. We were already a group apart and tried to defend our privileges. The train hurtled North for Lafia and Kaduna where we would change line for the train going to the West and Lagos. I had made this journey once already and so we were old hands now.

But the joy of travelling in a special train compartment with students, boys and girls from the same school, was an experience I had never had before and it was intoxicating! The difficulties of the journey were no longer important as we hurtled on to the North.

Daybreak on day two was in the northern region of Nigeria after crossing the River Benue. Some hours later at Lafia, our train stopped to take on more coal fuel and to fill up with water. When the train moved off we noticed a second engine at the back of the train. I had not noticed that during my first trip because I was too scared to look out of the window. Now confident with all my newly found friends, I looked out of the window and noticed this second engine. I asked one of the senior students and he explained that the train had to climb a hill past Jos towards Kaduna. Because the power of the front engine was too small to pull the train up this hill, a second engine had been fitted behind to push and thus get the train over the hill. I watched in amazement as our train snaked through terrifying escarpments by rivers and bridges all the way to Kafanchan and finally Kaduna, where night fell on the second day. We ate our meals, each to his or her Jerry can. There was very little interchange between the first year boys and girls. This was probably because we were rather young, aged between twelve and fourteen years maximum. There was a lot of shunting of wagons in Kaduna, to move various coaches to the right lines. This time, the coach I was travelling in was clearly marked for King's College, Lagos, and Iddo station. We did not have to bother because it was now the responsibility of the stationmaster to make sure that this government coach reached its destination of Lagos safely.

What a difference the passing of an entrance examination can make to one's life! The next morning after leaving Kaduna, the geographical centre of Nigeria, we were heading South West to Yorubaland and Lagos. There was nothing special to report except vast areas of open and uninhabited land. Nigeria seemed such a huge and varied country. We rolled on through the third day without enthusiasm and simply waiting for journey's end. Our journey would last another day and in mid-afternoon of the fourth day, our train would pull into Iddo railway station. Everybody would scramble to the luggage compartment for our boxes. The local stationmaster would check each individual box against the tag it carried to make sure the right owner claimed it. It was all so correct and civilised. Looking back now, it was like watching a Second World War film, with people behaving correctly and talking their turn. All the King's College boys and Queen's College girls gathered at a given spot so that we could be counted and surprise, surprise – a government truck supplied by the Public Works Department, PWD, awaited us! It was a huge truck without seats and painted dark green in colour. On the side was painted in huge letters 'Don't Waste Water'. This was the publicity by the Nigerian government at that time, aimed at saving water. Older students promptly told us the truck was baptised 'Don't Waste Water' because it was ugly and uncomfortable. Nevertheless, there we were having arrived in reserved coaches, we now had government transport to take us to college premises. King's and Queen's Colleges were surely islands of privilege? I was quite glad to partake of this privilege. Later, this aspect of King's College in particular would rankle with the new rulers of Nigeria between the 1960s and 1980s and they would attempt to abolish King's College, as elitist and not in line with the aspirations of Nigeria.

The children of the new rulers were unable to pass the entrance examinations for entering King's College and so it was said that it had to be closed! Luckily, a number of prominent old King's College students like former vice president Ekwueme, Ayida, Asiodu and others fought against that and saved King's College.

When our PWD truck arrived at the school premises later that evening, the house masters and prefects were there to receive us. They needed to because we really were like orphans going to orphanages to be looked after. Our names were read out, our school houses were announced and we followed the appropriate house prefect who led us to our individual dormitories. In the dormitories we were assigned our beds with a small locker by the side. We were instructed to empty our belongings into our lockers and then shown round the dormitories, the shower rooms, toilets, dining room, you name it. We were then brought back to the dormitories and an inventory of all the clothing including bed sheets and pillows – all white – was made. They had to be all there. After this, an older student showed us, probably a first year 'fag', how to make our bed. Bed was essentially three bare planks placed side by side on top of two trestles. One trestle was at the head and the other at the foot of the bed. I think there was some kind of blanket cover over the planks to soften the harshness, and you simply put your white bed sheet over this, but carefully tucked in at the corners. On top of your bed were two pillows that were supplied by the school. You had to supply your own white pillowcases. There was also a top white bed sheet to cover your body that had to be tucked carefully at the corners.

I think we were allowed to cover the white bed sheets with a coverlet, usually a piece of cloth wrapper common among males in southern Nigeria. Your cupboard contained clothing and various school items like books, but no food. You were severely punished if the prefect found biscuits, drinks, or anything edible in your cupboard. The first night as a boarder at King's College was a nightmare and I was excited and terrified. They rang bells for everything and you had to know where to go. That first night after showering and putting our boxes away, dinner was served at 7 p.m. The bell rang and every child rushed into the dining room and took the place assigned to him. Everybody seemed to be talking at the same time. The older students wanted to discuss their Christmas vacation with their friends. You had to be seated when a second and final bell sounded ten minutes later. The last people to come in would be the school prefects and the school captain. When the captain came in, everybody stopped talking and stood up. He would walk the full length of the dining room to the head table where the other prefects sat. The new boys were dispersed at all the tables so that we got to know the older students. When I arrived at King's College in 1950, people like Ekwueme who later became a vice-president of Nigeria under Shagari's Government was a prefect. Ayida, Asiodu, Akpofure and Oldman Hart from Port Harcourt were prefects in my first year at King's. Asiodu and Ayida were later to become super permanent secretaries to various Nigerian governments after independence. After everyone was seated, the captain stood up and everyone else also did. The school captain offered a prayer in English and everyone else chanted 'Amen' in unison and sat down. Almost simultaneously all the students seemed to turn over their plates.

Our plates were turned over to prevent flies landing onto the side in which food was served. The stewards had already left the day's meal in huge vats at the head of each table. A student was asked to serve up the meal into each student's plate that we passed round. My favourite meal was rice with fried plantains *dodo* and with a meat stew to eat it with. Water was served from huge jugs into glasses and everybody ate correctly with knives and forks. A number of kids had never used them before coming to King's College and they learnt by just watching other kids. For desserts we had either bananas or oranges. The oranges were sour and did not contain much juice. Our diet was well balanced and we had plenty to eat, so much so that most new adolescents changed and were unrecognisable after six months at King's College. Settling in was over a weekend in January.

On the Monday after, we went in for our first classes and met our class teachers for the first time. The first night was the night when we, the new students, had to be introduced to the older students or boarders in what was known as the initiation ceremony. A bell rang at about 8.30 p.m. and we all gathered in the assembly hall in our sports wear – khaki shorts or trousers and khaki shirts. The school captain announced to the assembled hall of about 300 students that there were new arrivals, or 'Fags' in the community and that we had to introduce ourselves. The first thing we were taught by one of the minders was our 'anthem' of fagship. We were taught to repeat to all present – that is, to everyone from Class 2 to the Sixth Form: 'I am a fag, I am to be seen and not to be heard.' That recitation terrified us and put us in our place.

After this group avowal of our nothingness, we were required individually to introduce ourselves to the whole community. Each little boy of twelve to thirteen years old stood up alone and had to tell the gathered borders his full name, his village of origin and then to sing a song or dance or play a musical instrument. For those of us who were shy and who had never before spoken in public, this was truly an ordeal. The older students were awful and baited us. If you came from a well-known town like Onitsha or Ibadan, Abeokuta or Aba, that was all right. But if you said you came from Awomama or Ogbomosho or some other little known town or village, the whole hall exploded in laughter of derision. You had come from the bush and you had to be 'civilised'. Our rendition of traditional village songs from our little communities did not save us either. You have to remember that we all came from different ethnic groups and spoke different languages. Any of these songs would in any case sound weird to people from the other tribes or ethnic groups. And that was the whole point of King's College. Twelve and thirteen year olds from different parts of Nigeria were going to be made to live together and to respect and understand each other! And it really worked!

The first lesson in this transformation was that, from the initiation night, we were to be known only by our surnames. We no longer had our first or Christian names. And so, everyone knew me as Ibekwe. Following closely on that was a total interdiction of speaking in your native language or vernacular. It was a serious offence punishable by a prefect if you spoke in the vernacular. Other pupils could report you. This had the amazing effect of detribalising us. We all became Nigerians and not Igbos, Hausas or Yorubas. Mind you, I do not remember any Hausa colleagues from the North at this time. I had a classmate from the Middle Belt, Victor Archer, later known as Victor Ndalugi of UBA Bank. Many northerners subsequently came to King's after I had left. Punishment for a serious school offence varied and you could for instance be made to copy out 500 lines of Shakespeare or asked to write 500 times 'I must not speak vernacular in school premises' and you had to submit that before a given time to the school prefect. If you failed to carry out your punishment you would be reported to the school captain and from then on it could snowball to the house master, then to the principal and caning! We passed our night of initiation credibly. The older students had laughed at us. That was our payment for our rights of passage. We had been admitted into the student body and that was very important because that would form the centre of our lives for the next seven years. At the end of our initiation ceremony, a few of the old hands were called in to entertain us and they were magical. There was Ogunleye who sang jazz classics such as

'Oklahoma 2251' and 'Kalamazoo' about trains with all the puffs, etc. He was the best and continued to entertain with this refrain on Sundays for years until he left King's College.

After the initiation, the bells for junior lights out sounded at about 9.25 p.m. We were all in our dormitories, which were assigned to us according to the houses we belonged to. There were four houses named after former English teachers in the school. There was Hyde Johnson House, the most successful house in sports; then Harman House to which I belonged; Mckee-Wright House and Payne House. We all had healthy rivalry between the houses and that was the chief motivating factor for all our competitions.

At 9.30 p.m. the second bell went for junior lights out and we all crashed with a resounding noise on our beds. There was not a sound anywhere. Senior students (Class 4 to 6) were to repeat this one hour later at 10.30 p.m. for senior lights out. And so ended my first day at King's College. The next day would be Monday and we would start early with the wake-up bell at about 6.30 a.m.

Everything seemed to be regulated by bells. We went in for cold showers at between 6.30 and 7.00 a.m. and dressed up in our splendid white uniforms. We made our beds and went in for a breakfast of porridge, tea and bread soon afterwards. Another bell signalled the end of breakfast time and the stand by our beds for inspection by the house prefects. Our dormitories were swept, dusted and cleaned for inspection every day. In addition to that, some of us had the extra task of cleaning the dormitories, corridors and bathrooms. I do not remember who cleaned the toilets. Some boys who were more fortunate were selected by house captains to be their fags, responsible for washing their underpants and cleaning their shoes. To qualify, you had to be cute and good-looking! There was no evidence of homosexual behaviour at King's but many of the senior boys were 'in love' with young and rather pretty little boys. You knew something was up when at lunch or dinner, a steward would suddenly arrive at your table and present you on a plate or fork, a piece of meat, donated by some older student from either the top table or from another table. The steward would graciously announce to you that your present was from 'so-and-so'.

The poor young student would blush and really look uncomfortable while everybody else would grin. I myself was a recipient of some favours, but gave nothing in return. In addition to that I was the fag of the school and Nigerian 440 yards race champion, A K Amu. He liked me and I admired him so much. This admiration was to lead me subsequently to take athletics seriously and to win the school long jump championships in 1955.

At 8.30 a.m. we had to be in the main school assembly hall for the first day of school and also to see the school masters. Up till now, we had seen the house master, Mr J P Savage, and his assistant, Mr A J Enyeazu who was also the assistant sports master. Both were Nigerians – Africans. The school assembly on the other hand, the next morning was quite something. The school assembled in lines, by classes, the sixth forms in front and us the newest behind. The teachers, mostly English, filed in, including a woman, a Mrs Butterfield, who was to become our English teacher. I believe there was another female teacher. There were a couple of African teachers, but the Europeans were in the majority. Every male teacher wore impeccably ironed and starched clothes with a tie. Every teacher wore a black graduate gown. This was impeccable. There was total silence as the school organist/pianist (I think it was one of the Akinreles) in a starched white suit and the blue and white striped King's College tie, with the school badge attached, marched to the front to sit on his piano seat. One minute later, a very tall man, certainly two metres tall, marched into the hall wearing a black academic gown and with a sweeping flow of his left arm. His strides were long, swift and decisive.

His face was beautifully tanned as he climbed two or three steps to the stage of the assembly hall. From there he imperiously announced the school song for that morning. The pianist struck the first few bars and the whole school exploded into song in a melodious and obviously already rehearsed manner. I think we sang three stanzas and stopped.

This man who had breezed in was the school principal, Mr J R Bunting, MA Oxon. He was everything you expected of the English school establishment – flashing blue eyes, arrogant, self-assured and clearly sent by his majesty's government to build a boarding school in Africa in the image of British boarding schools, and my God, they were succeeding! When the singing stopped, Mr Bunting spoke to the assembly with a voice that seemed to tremble. I do not think it was due to fear but more of authority because everyone, including the teachers, was terrified of him. I think it was an act he put on!

He welcomed the new students and read out a whole series of instructions. At the same time he reminded us of the uniqueness of our position. When the assembly ended, we went back to our classrooms and our lockers. Everyone had a classroom and a locker, but you had to leave your classroom for certain lessons. The day started with us being introduced to various teachers and being given our timetables. Lessons lasted 45 minutes each. There were three lessons in the morning that took us to about midday. There was a short break at midday and classes continued later, to about 1.30 p.m., when the school day ended.

Our teachers left for their residences in the leafy suburbs of Ikoyi where the expatriates lived. Day students left the school compound to catch local buses to take them to suburbs like Obalende, Idumota and Yaba. Those of us who were boarders headed for the dormitories and at 2.00 p.m. the bells sounded again, this time for lunch. We piled in, sat at our designated places. The school prefects marched in, followed by the school captain. We all rose up, prayers were said and we charged at our food. We were so hungry. The meal was one or the other of the staple diets of rice and dodo (fried plantain) or rice with black-eyed beans, or yam with dodo, etc. I was glad to have such a good meal. And on top of that, you could have ice water to drink. It was so hot. Several years later, this diet would become monotonous and unappealing.

We would finish our lunch in a hurry and retire to our dormitories for an afternoon siesta that was compulsory. This lasted from I think 2.30 to 3.15 p.m. with the whole compound of 300 students completely silent in mid-afternoon. At the end of the siesta we were all awakened by yet another bell. Everyone hurriedly changed into khaki shirts and shorts for sports. Sports and personal hobbies like boy scouts, photography, fishing, etc., were practised every day between 3.30 p.m. and 6.30 p.m. These were organised in one-hour shifts because of lack of playing fields. The teachers who we had seen earlier in the day in ties all turned up in shorts or trousers and without ties. The temperature at 4.00 p.m. in Lagos was still around 28°C, with very high humidity.

Our European teachers were red and perspired like they were going to collapse. But they held on well and taught us a whole variety of games. We had football, cricket, hockey, tennis, squash, athletics and even swimming, which had to be done in the municipal pools at Onikan. Of course, the most popular games were football and cricket. Those who excelled in both like the Nkune brothers from Calabar and the Akpata brothers from Benin were the stars of the school. Principal Bunting and the history master, Davis, were particularly keen on cricket and they actually formed a joint school and staff cricket team that played against established cricket clubs in Lagos. I was good at football and quickly got into the junior football team, called 'the Mosquitoes'. The story goes that I used to literally fly down the left wing chasing the balls that had been crossed to me from the centre forward position. From this exploit I got the nickname Atinkpala which apparently was the Yoruba name for a sort of gazelle that had extremely thin legs and looked as if it was in flight when it ran! With time, I added tennis, squash and athletics to my repertoire, making me an invaluable reserve on school team outings where several sports were to be played. As my School Leaving Certificate would say in 1956, 'He represented his school in all sports without being outstanding'! Some European wives accompanied their husbands to the school compound in the evening when they came to supervise sports. That gave us the chance to see their lifestyles. Mrs Bunting was very stylishly dressed and, in a way, pretty. There were rumours that she was older than our principal, Mr Bunting.

Rumour also had it that they had come from Jamaica in the British West Indies where they had also run a government boarding school. Mrs Bunting was forbidding and the other expatriate wives seemed in awe of her. She was said to be the 'other eye' of the principal and reported everything that was out of place to her husband. We also noted that the only student that she regularly spoke to was Jibowu, who was the classmate of people like Chigbo, Maduka, Adeyinka, who were later to become my close friends over the years. Everyone knew that Jibowu had the ear of Mrs Bunting and so was afraid that he passed on every school gossip to her. So people were careful with him. The other teachers' wives, like Mrs Kellet, the wife of the geography teacher, or Mrs Thomas, the wife of the chemistry teacher, were very kind and not too young. By contrast, the wives of some of the younger teachers were quite attractive but strangely did not make any impression on us. I think we were respectful and felt it would not be correct to be attracted to your teacher's wife.

Mrs Perkins, the wife of the vice-principal, was strikingly attractive and much younger than her husband. It was her second marriage – or so we supposed. She used to accompany her husband on dormitory inspections well after midnight. The summer months in Lagos were hot and torrid. To cool off at night, some of the older boys slept in the raw, with only a coverlet and no pyjamas. They often lost this cover at night and Mrs Perkins' eyes were exposed to things she was not supposed to see. Younger expatriate teachers like Davis and Mancroft were handsome bachelors and we were convinced that some of the wives who came for sports in the evening, came to admire and probably lust after them on the sports field.

By about 6.00 p.m. the sun would start dipping into the horizon and all the sports would come to a stop and everyone would pack up to go home. Teachers went back to Ikoyi and day students went out of the premises for buses to take them to Lagos suburbs. The boarders like me went for showers and changed after that into dry Khaki uniforms for evening meal. This duly took place at 7.00 p.m. following the same rituals, and would end at about 7.30 p.m. for evening studies to start. These studies were individual affairs in which you took your books to your classroom and revised what you had learnt during the day. One does not need much imagination to know that this was very unpopular. Class prefects who sat in the teachers' chairs supervised it. We had to study at night with the whole school lit up every night except Saturdays and Sundays.

An occasional mosquito would buzz into life, causing an

almighty clap by a student trying to kill it. Everybody's composure would be disturbed and people would attempt to talk, with a resounding 'silence' echoed by the class prefect. This ordeal would end by about 9.00 p.m. giving the junior classes just 30 minutes until lights out at 9.30 p.m. We, the new ones, all quietly tripped out after evening studies and walked over the sports field to our dormitories to get ready for bed. It was the first time in the whole day we had been together on our own. We exchanged a few words and by and large seemed pleased with how things had gone. Benjamin, Benji, my classmate from Aba, was well above all this adjustment. It was as if being at King's College was the most natural thing for him. If King's College had a kindergarten school, you felt that Benji should have been in there as well!

And so our first day ended beautifully, in bed at 9.30 p.m. We were all asleep by 10.00 p.m. because I do not remember hearing the noise of the seniors going to bed at 10 p.m. And thus ended my first full school day of classes at King's College in January 1950. This routine was so repeated over and over again that it became literally part of one's life. Waking up early in the morning to go for cold showers in the dark and cleaning dormitory corridors in near darkness were routine from Monday to Friday. The food was the same, although there were changes on a day-to-day basis. The combination I disliked the most was beans and yam on Tuesdays, and so Tuesdays became dark days for me. Black–eyed beans were served on Thursdays as well, with fish. The beans were riddled with weevils and so a popular pastime on beans' night was to count how many weevils you got for the day. On Friday evenings everyone had to send their week's dirty laundry to be cleaned. This was a major logistics exercise. Every student filled out a form for clothes he sent for cleaning for the week – three white shirts, two white trousers, four khaki shorts, one bed sheet, etc. The clothes and filled-out sheets of paper were handed in on Friday evening after meals to a steward in charge of laundry. Professional cleaners who worked for the school cleaned them. That was why our clothes were so incredibly white and brought us the envy of other schools like Lagos Grammar School. Friday signalled the end of the week when everything could go at a slower tempo. Even the study classes on Friday nights were a bit relaxed. We were allowed to go into town on Saturdays, after breakfast. To do so, you had to obtain an *exeat* from the house master stating the purpose of your visit and how long you would be out for.

On some evenings, we could go to the cinema using part of our pocket money of one shilling per week. To go to the cinema, you had to have several boys interested, and we went into town in single file. We did not have to wear our school uniforms to go to the cinema, but for all other outings you were required to wear your school uniform with your badge attached. This had a double advantage: for one you were constrained to behave yourself in town because everyone knew you were from King's College. The second advantage was that people showed you consideration and respect because you were from the premier secondary school of Nigeria. The outings during the week introduced me to the joys of polyphoto which were small passport-size pictures in black and white that you got two minutes after they were taken. I also tasted my first ice cream, which was Walls ice cream from Kingsway, Marina Lagos. This was the supermarket where the expatriates shopped and in those days it belonged to Unilever (United Africa Company), more like Woolworth's of the UK, and had everything – from imported clothing and shoes to local chicken and eggs. Going to Kingsway department store was a good outing.

Saturday was the day when you did your thing. There was no compulsory entertainment in the evening. Sunday was a different story. The morning started with a superb breakfast of Quaker Oats porridge, followed by nicely fried eggs washed down with cocoa containing a lot of milk. This breakfast was so delicious that people made deals during the week to swap their eggs for other peoples' fried plantain or meat during the week. Sunday breakfast remained ingrained in me as what King's College was all about, and I was not alone. There was nothing compulsory to do after this leisurely breakfast that incidentally was one hour later, (about 8.30 a.m.) than during the week.

After this pleasant breakfast, we had to see to our souls, something taken very seriously at the school. Our religious upbringing was extremely important in much the same way as it was regarded in England. After breakfast, dressed in our full white regalia, Protestants went to service in the Anglican chapel at King's College. Catholics went to a 10.30 a.m. mass at the Holy Cross cathedral in Lagos, a stone throw from the school compound. Muslims did not go anywhere, but would perform their rites in full when the feast of the Ramadan would be celebrated.

And so you had in this school the foundations of religious tolerance which Nigerian society and for that matter some European societies like in the Balkans have never succeeded in putting in place. We were taught to respect and value as of the same weight the other people's religions. I liked going to mass at Holy Cross cathedral because we were like prisoners let out for the day. We usually went in a single file under the control of a school prefect. Once mass ended, we filed out again to return to our boarding house. Lunch on Sundays was another delight. This time, we had Jollof rice, which is a kind of local paella rice. This was served with fried chicken in a delicious sauce. If you had pocket money, you could purchase a bottle of Coca Cola. This was heaven because we were living a life way above those of most children in Nigeria, including kids from wealthy families. After this sumptuous lunch we would retire for siesta at about 2.00 p.m. to get up at 3.00 p.m. Sunday afternoons were free days where you could wear your own dress and not the school uniform. The local students, mostly Yorubas born in Lagos, would put on very beautiful and lavish dresses.

Those of us from the East could not afford these and just loped around in our khaki clothes. Sunday was also special because we were allowed visitors from 4.00 p.m. to 6.00 p.m. To receive them, you had to inform the house master in advance so that the school knew who was entering the premises and appropriate instructions given to the gate man to let them in. Once again, the Easterners had few visitors and I for one did not receive anybody for the five of my seven years at King's College. In the sixth and seventh years I had two different girlfriends who visited me, but that later. For those of us who did not have Sunday visitors, we frankly did not give a hoot. We looked down our noses at parents who came to see their sons. Invariably we considered them to be less educated than their kids who were with us. And even where the father was a barrister or a doctor, we at King's were sure we would achieve their status and therefore had no need to kow-tow to them. The only visitor that made any impression on me was the Oni of Ife who came to see his two sons, the Aderemis, one of whom was my classmate. This important Yoruba monarch arrived in his Rolls Royce car and in accordance with Yoruba culture his two sons went flat on their faces in the reception room to kiss his feet. I was impressed by this but later teased the younger Aderemi on why he had to kiss his old man's feet in public! Bells rang out at end of visitors' period and you would see these disconsolate parents leave their wards again in the quiet sobriety of King's College. As far as we were concerned, the outside world was nothing but chaos.

The end of Sunday would signal the beginning of another tough week. As a consequence, I have had all my life a horror of Sunday evenings. Dinner was fried plantain (dodo) and rice and very popular. But for reasons that still escape me, the plantains they fried for us on Sunday evenings always seemed to be too ripe and soggy. After the evening meals we would assemble in the school hall to learn school songs – to be sung the next week at assembly. This was a grim exercise which frankly I detested. There was a master who taught us and occasionally we learnt other English folk songs. At the end of the songs we would have house entertainment. For those of us who were shy or were not very good at remembering songs, you simply prayed that the prefect did not pick on you to come up and entertain the whole school. You have to remember that it was now about 8.00 to 8.30 p.m. and all you really wanted was to be left alone to get yourself ready for Monday. I must have been called up some time but I do not have any memory of this. There were some regulars, though, who always seemed to have some nice song or bit of theatre to entertain us. Our favourite was always our man with 'Chattanooga Choo Choo' and 'Pennsylvania 6500'. He was the star and if he sang we went back to the dormitories happy and contented. At the end of the evening's entertainment, we would return to the dormitories to collect our cleaned laundry for the week. Bedtime for juniors was at 9.30 and at 10.00 p.m. for seniors and so the week ended and Monday would start again the next day. Generally we slept well without interference from mosquitoes. Our dormitories were fumigated every night before we slept and our windows were wide open so that a constant stream of air prevented mosquitoes from biting us.

Our lives in the first term settled into a pleasant routine and going to classes was only a matter of crossing over from the boarding houses to the classrooms, a distance of a hundred metres. The wide variety of subjects was both a fascination and a challenge. In those days, Nigerian schools and in particular the accredited colleges prepared their students for the Cambridge School Certificate and the Cambridge Higher School Certificate examinations on the same basis as students in England. In our first year, there were sixty new students divided into two classes. I was in class 1B in January 1950 with twenty-nine other kids. I was to find out later on that a number of the new entrants had done so well in their entrance examinations they had won scholarships worth about £40 per annum to attend King's College. And so my rank and position was well and clearly established. Not only did I not have a scholarship but also I was in the B or second stream selected for 1950. I was among my intellectual superiors and this was to condition my attitude and redouble the efforts I put into my studies in the first two years of my stay at King's College. Seven years later, I was to have the second best result for the whole of Nigeria in the Higher School Certificate examination, second only to Femi Sowemimo, later a professor at the Lagos school of medicine. The subjects we were taught in the first year were English, History, Geography, Latin, Mathematics, Physics, Biology, and Chemistry.

School Masters at King's College

A good school is often the result of good teachers. King's College was in this sense very lucky and exceptional. We had very good teachers, both English and Nigerian. Our English teacher was a Mrs Butterfield whose husband was a captain in the British army and had been seconded to Nigeria. There was also a wiry little teacher from the then Gold Coast, Mr S A Winful, who also assisted Mrs Butterfield in English. We the students thought this poor fellow was in love with Mrs Butterfield because each time he had to mention her name, he fluffed and said the most stupid things like 'Did Mrs Butterfly sorry Mrs Butterfly, sorry Mrs Butterfield?' If anybody laughed he would tell the student that he was possessed by the devil which he said came from thinking about women. He would then drift into a monologue of how he was also possessed by the devil as a young man and what he did to get rid of the devil. I think he was slightly deranged. He always appeared to grind his teeth, probably because of badly fitted dentures. In addition to English, Winful also taught Divinity, which gave him the excuse to talk incessantly about the devil. He seemed to derive a vicarious pleasure by being explicit in describing his past sexual escapades to fifteen-year-old boys at a boarding school! Like all male teachers, S A Winful also supervised games. He made a further name for himself by falling asleep while supervising a boxing match. He was sat on a high stool, fell asleep and subsequently fell off his chair. The boxing contest had to be restarted.

A regular feature of our English classes whenever Mrs Butterfield taught us was that one of my classmates, Adebayo, would drop his lead pencil on the wooden floor and this would make quite a bit of noise. Adebayo was small and so always sat in the front row. He would then bend down to collect his pencil and at the same time attempt to look up at the skirt of Mrs Butterfield. This happened whenever Mrs Butterfield was seated in the teacher's chair, which was much higher than those of the pupils. Mrs Butterfield would leave her seat, walk up to Adebayo and grab him by one of his ears and twist it while shouting 'naughty boy'. We all laughed and knew it would happen again the week after.

In addition to these two English teachers, there was a half-mad Irishman, Michael Kevin Flannagan who we called Aggresso because he always seemed so aggressive. He taught English literature to the older classes and was apparently a very good violinist. He made whole classes listen to classical music for 40 minutes at a time and taught several generations of Nigerians the beauty of Shakespeare. He put on many plays in the school, including T S Elliot's *Murder in the Cathedral*. There was a story by the class above mine which recalls that Aggresso was once leading their class in song. He took a deep breath, raised both arms to conduct the class and his shorts promptly fell down. He had no underpants! Later the boys discussed at length whether it was true that all white males were less endowed than them in that area.

For history in the senior classes, we had R M Elphick, a British aristocrat who looked and behaved the part. His accent was cut-glass Oxford and he did not mix too much with the other teachers. Philip Davis taught history to school certificate level and his nickname was Moldavia because he was very keen on the history of Central Europe in the nineteenth century. He would become principal of King's College some years later. He was the classical Englishman – tall, blond, handsome, single, with the whitest shirts and shorts worn over white knee-length socks and the best-polished black shoes you ever saw. He walked with a military gait because he had been a captain in the British Army.

The Geography teacher for the lower school was Mr Kellett, a gentle old soul who will be remembered for running into our geography class in 1952 with tears in his eyes and announcing to the class that 'His Majesty, King George the VI died peacefully in his bed from Coronary Thrombosis'. The death of the king of course was sad news because Nigeria was still a British colony and many of us in class knew about what the King had done during the war that had just ended. But Nigerian kids did not expect a teacher, let alone an expatriate one, to cry. We were embarrassed, and nobody knew what coronary thrombosis was or dared to ask.

W A Perkins also taught Geography, but to the senior school. WAP, as he was called, would later become the principal when J R Bunting was sent to the Ministry of Education. W A Perkins was so sure of himself that he would reply to a question in the Geography class by saying, 'I do not know the answer and nobody else knows.' It was said later after our school days that probably Perkins' briefing on Nigeria before he came out was that Nigerians despised ignorance. He therefore did not want his pupils to laugh at him by his confessing ignorance on any issue. He was said to have told one of the senior classes that he was the 'first in the first class' in his degree examination. Perkins was a dapper and very well-turned-out classic Englishman. This was to pay off nicely for him, because he divorced his ageing wife and remarried a very young and attractive English woman. Perkins and his young wife were out every Saturday night at one dance ball or another in Ikoyi or Yaba dressed in white tuxedo and his wife in beautiful flowing robes.

For Latin we had an African, Mr George Percy Savage, later a vice-principal. He was what was called in those days a Brazilian Nigerian. Another African, Mr Bestman ('Don't Confuse Me') taught mathematics and Physics, assisted by a younger and much cleverer African, Mr Ibi Mboto from Ogoja. Mr Mboto was a real odd ball. He was stocky with enormous thigh and shoulder muscles. He spoke with a high-pitched voice at great speed and kept to himself. He created and ran the photographic club for profit, all of which he ploughed back into the club. He took all the pictures on King's College in this book. He was a brilliant Physics teacher. Many years later, the University of Lagos awarded him an honorary doctorate degree in Physics, by appreciative former students led by Professor Seriki of the University of Lagos who died in January 2002. Bestman later changed his name to Ajumogobia and I believe returned to his native Rivers Province as Nigeria increasingly began to revert to tribalism. He also died in a plane crash near Lagos in the early 1990s, aged 80 years.

Our Biology teacher was a young Englishman who had literally just come down from Cambridge, Mr John Marcroft. John was young, shy and good-looking and was to become a personal friend when I reached the sixth form. He would often take me with him to go shopping at Kingsway for his food at the time in the afternoon when everyone was having siesta. Of course that did not go down well with the rest of my classmates, who labelled me a creep.

For Chemistry we had the venerable, beloved and frightening Welshman, Mr W G Thomas, who spoke with the broadest Welsh-accented English you ever heard. The senior boys joked about Mr Thomas and we would later pick this up. But nobody dared joke in front of him or answer him back. If someone broke a beaker in the chemistry lab, Mr Thomas would yell out to ask what the noise was about. The class would freeze in fear, as a timid little voice from the class would say something like, 'It is a beaker that fell, sir.'

Thomas would reply, 'The beaker does not walk. You pushed it over, imbecile.' The whole class would explode with laughter and Thomas would immediately instruct us to stop giggling and to concentrate on our laboratory experiments. His nickname was 'Palita' because of the exaggerated way he pronounced 'per litre' with his broad Welsh accent.

On another occasion, the following dialogue occurred in a Chemistry laboratory class between Thomas and a student:

Thomas: 'What was the colour of the precipitate in your beaker?'

Student: 'Yellow, sir.'

Thomas: 'Your brain matter is yellow.'

On another occasion, Thomas asked a student in a laboratory class what he had observed in an experiment requiring water to be distilled from a mixture. The boy replied, 'The water rose up and ran.' Even Thomas laughed! Despite our fear, virtually every boy in the Science class of 1955, the class above mine, went to him for school-leaving testimonials. Typical of him, he asked one student, ' Am I the only science teacher in this school?'

W G Thomas was by far the best teacher I have ever had in my life and he taught me to like chemistry. And once he thought you were able, he supported and cajoled you to the end. I remember getting the results of some tests we had done in one of the junior

My parents' wedding day, Aba – 1935

Papa, Gabriel Ibekwe, Aba – 1942

Mama, Theresa Ibekwe, Aba –1952

Uncle Joe (right) with Dr E Njaka, Port Harcourt – 1947

Aba Town Council meeting with British Resident, Owerri Province, Aba – 1949

George Spiropoulous, Aba – 1952

Author, first year student, King's College, Lagos – 1950

King's College, Lagos, new wing – 1952

Author – third year student, King's College, Lagos – 1952

School photograph, King's College, Lagos – 1955

King's College, Lagos, Athletics Team – 1955

Receiving the Long Jump Trophy, King's College, Lagos, Inter-house Sports – 1955

*Sir John Macpherson, Nigeria Governor General, and W A Perkins, Principal
King's College – 1955*

Typical Sunday evening, King's College gardens, Lagos – 1955

Dressed to march past Queen Elizabeth II, Lagos Race Course – 1956

Queen Elizabeth II and Prince Phillip, Youth Rally, Lagos Race Course – 1956

Dinner at King's College, Lagos, after Youth Rally for Queen Elizabeth II – 1956

Old wing, King's College, Lagos, floodlit for Queen Elizabeth II's visit – 1956

Nigerian Broadcasting Service, Lagos, Cricket Team – 1957

Cricket match, Lagos Race Course, Major J C Allen at wicket – 1957

King's College Straw Club (1956 Alumni) Meeting – 1958

Author, leaving Lagos for University of Manchester, England – 1958

Benji Maduka, University of Heidelberg, Germany – 1958

Author – first year student, University of Manchester (UMIST), Hulme Hall of Residence – 1958

Vicky and George Spiropoulos – Lagos, 2000

Dr Gilbert Chigbo – Akokwa, 2005

classes and he walked up to me to ask how well I had done. I showed him my results and he literally asked me if I had been asleep during the test, with a further remark that I was far better than I had scored in that test. That really fired me up and I never looked back, leading finally to a PhD in Chemistry from Manchester University ten years later.

The most enduring memories of those days were the nicknames we had for masters and students, and the prank, students played on masters. One prank that was told to me by Chigbo from the class above me involved poor Bestman, the Physics teacher. Bestman was struggling with the solution to a physics problem on the black board. He finished the calculation and the answer he got was less by the number two than what it should have been. A. K. Amu, the athletics champion shouted from the back of the class 'Plus two sir'. Bestman added two, got the right answer and then sat down beaming to the class. Next was 'Please sir,' from A K Amu, who then asked Bestman, 'Where did you get the two from, sir?' The class collapsed laughing. But it was not just the masters who gaffed. In one physics laboratory class, Ibi Mboto asked a student 'Why does a ruler appear bent when half immersed in water?' One bright spark from the back of the class replied, 'Because gravity is pulling it down in one half and up-thrust is pushing it up on the other half.'

On another occasion, the same A K Amu asked the English teacher, E J Moses, a Sierra Leonean from Foura Bay College, to help him in the pronunciation of certain words like 'run, rain, ran'. Moses, like all Sierra Leoneans, could not pronounce 'R' normally and was way down to 'Ran' before he caught on.

We had more English than African teachers at the time I attended King's College. The African teachers were, without exception, young university graduates who had just returned from the United Kingdom. The younger English teachers also had to get used to us. By and large it went well because the sports field was a wonderful place to get to know people. I threw myself with enthusiasm into everything. It was as if I had finally found a place where I could grow and let my imagination take flight. For the next few months we would settle down to school wonderfully. We would go to classes every day and if you were ill you had the school nurse to recommend medicines or confinement or visit to the general hospital which was not far from us in Broad Street.

Finished were my father's special purgative days. This new regime of balanced diets and regular exercise meant that if you could not be in class you had better have a document from the medical people to explain your absence. In addition to a wide variety of sports activities, every Wednesday afternoon was dedicated to hobbies and my God, there were so many. For these, a number of teachers and their wives played very active parts. The hobbies available were all made into clubs and so we had a whole variety including: fishing club, dramatic society, the school choir, the debating society, boy scouts, army cadets club, photographic society, etc. We were very subtly being introduced in Nigeria, to the same past times as the English middle-class children in boarding schools in England.

Daily Life as a Boarder

Student life as a boarder at King's College was busy and very fulfilling. I cannot say as much for the day students. The poor sods spent half the morning catching buses from all parts of Lagos and usually arrived sweaty, dishevelled and smelly. Their white uniforms were often soiled and more often than not they arrived late to class. On top of that, many would fall asleep in class because they probably had not had a decent night's sleep, what with the heat, noise and overcrowding of most of Lagos. They were a class apart, irrespective of their seniority in class.

For boarders, life on the school premises was truly wonderful. We spent all our time with kids who thought like us, behaved in accordance with certain norms. A former King's College student, who later became head of the Nigerian television authority, recently said that King's College in our era produced a bunch of kids who were idealists and totally unprepared for the rough and tumble, and corruption of Nigerian society, which they were supposed to lead. Still, it was better to produce decent young men, even if later the price they had to pay to integrate into Nigerian society would be high. The routine of daily life as a boarder was mainly going to classes and playing sports, five days a week. It was therefore no surprise, especially in the first year, that we looked forward to the first break of this relentless schedule. This would come with the first vacation in 1950 and would be the Easter holiday. The first term ended around April for the Easter holiday of 1950. The break was very welcome.

For students like myself from the East – the 'Igbo boys', as we were called – we had to stay in Lagos, on the school premises. The government would give us a warrant to travel home once a year but that would be for the long vacation in July. The effect of this on our morale was terrible. At the beginning of the vacation period, the school shut down and the local fellows, mostly Yorubas, went off to be with their parents in Abeokuta, Ibadan, and Ilorin – all not very far away.

Those of us left behind, mostly the Easterners – Igbo, Rivers, Calabar people, etc. – felt like orphans. We had nowhere to go to and nobody would come to visit us or take us away. So we organised games like table tennis, or long marches to Kuramo Waters where the Atlantic Ocean crashed into the rocks off Lagos. Some of us went to cinemas in groups and later on when we were older we would actually go to a dance hall on Sundays, to Yaba at Bobby Bensons's club which was popularly known as Sunday Mass. A skeleton staff of cooks and stewards stayed behind to cook and feed us, but everything was on a reduced scale and time was very elastic. This enforced isolation was later to form a strong bond between those of us, the Easterners, who stayed behind. It also made us very resilient and independent because we had to survive as kids, all be it privileged, in Lagos, the capital of Nigeria. It was no secret that we were all relieved when the two weeks holiday ended and school resumed.

My second term at King's College would start after Easter in late April 1950. Boarders came back a day before and assembled as usual for evening meals. This was a chance to exchange stories with friends on what we had been up to during the break. Most of our teachers had also not gone back to England. Some teachers stayed behind in Lagos or went across to Cameroon or Gold Coast for a little break or simply swam in the creeks around Lagos. Our expatriate teachers had the same constraints that we had. They could only travel back to England once a year on government warrants. There was no question of them travelling back to England under their own steam. It was long (by boat) and very expensive. You have to remember, the Second World War had just ended five years earlier. People like Marcroft had come out to the colonies to help us, for sure, but also to make a living. He wore the same heavy shoes every day, morning and afternoon, for about four years. His clothes looked as if they had been bought from an Army & Navy Store. The older and cheekier students like Akpata, teased and tormented him. For example, Marcroft always carried a torch with him at night and I remember Akpata asking him why he did so. Had his parents told him there was no electricity in Nigeria? Poor Marcroft would blush from ear to ear and not answer, but he was always generous in spirit.

He was thin and not very good at sports, but he was always there. He could not have been older than 25 years, but he was a good and dedicated teacher who in the end wanted the older boys as his friends. He was not much older than the ancient students, like Hart, we had at that time!

As soon as classes started in earnest, we plunged ourselves back into our studies. The assembly went on as usual and the school songs sounded even better as we began to join fully in all the activities. The only cloud on the horizon would be some serious examinations at the end of June 1950. These examination would be significant because they would give us the first clues on whether we would move on to a new class in the new year or be kicked out of King's College. April and May would go very quickly and June duly arrived. Sometime in mid-June the exams started. These were my first exams since getting into King's College. My results were encouraging, as I had scored higher than average marks. All that remained after passing our examinations was for our first long vacation. We started preparations by the end of June, immediately after we knew the examination results. We would not leave until mid-July but that was all that we talked about.

My First Long Vacation

For the new students like me, we had not seen our parents and family for six months already and for a thirteen/fourteen-year-old that is very difficult. School was wonderful but on the other hand it was like all institutions, a sort of prison. School formally closed at the end of June. The masters would leave for England by boat, on the Elder Dempster Lines, and we would not see them until September. The local Lagos boys and most of the Yoruba students from nearby towns would leave in the first days of July. Those of us who had some friends among them would exchange addresses and promise to write to each other during the holidays. For the Easterners, the Igbo, Calabar and Rivers folks, we would go East on a special coach reserved for King's and Queen's College students. For most of the first six months we had not heard or seen the Queen's College girls who had come with us in January. One or two days before the appointed day, we stayed up well into the night packing our things in our battered suitcases. With the little pocket money we had we bought biscuits, sardines, corned beef and orange squash to last us the journey of four days and three nights back to eastern Nigeria. This time our food would not rot like when we came from the East. The food now was all 'civilised' and pre-packed. None of it compared with my mama's stew. I made sure I packed my Jerry can for the return journey from Aba in September.

As expected, the Public Works Department truck arrived on time on the appointed day at King's College to take students to catch the train home. The driver of the truck called out the names of the first group to mount the truck with our luggage to Iddo railway station. The rest would come in another truck. As the truck pulled away from the school premises, there was a wonderful sense of joy. We were going home to our families and nothing could be more pleasant than that. We did not dislike our school or friends, or even Lagos; it was simply the joy of being reunited with our loved ones. The state of euphoria would continue all through our registration at Iddo and making our last purchases of sweet loaves of bread characteristic of Lagos. We would need that to eat with either the sardines or corned beef. Sometime while this was going on, the truck carrying Queen's College girls would arrive to join our train. Our coach was reserved in part for them. As they came into the compartments we noticed how much they had filled out. They were now real girls, some with fairly well-developed breasts. Of course we were interested and some flirting went on. The train pulled off after about an hour or so, to traverse in reverse the same journey and places I had passed in January getting to King's College, Lagos. But as always seems the case, the return journey seemed faster and sweeter. Before long we had passed Abeokuta on our way to Ibadan and Ilorin. We were in Western Nigeria and the next morning we would cross the Niger River at Jebba and head for Northern Nigeria and the savannah. We had seen this vegetation and landscape before and so we were not very interested. Instead we spent a lot of time exchanging addresses with our colleagues in order to be able to contact them during the three months vacation. Addresses such as, 'c/o CMS Church, Main Market, Aguleri' were not uncommon. A lot of the students from the East turned out to be the proverbial bright boys from tiny villages that were not even on the map. They had made it to King's College by dint of hard work and some brightness and certainly had not come from any wealth or privilege. Most of them had come from villages without post offices.

By contrast I came from Aba, a busy commercial and administrative centre and my address, appropriately, was P O Box 140, Aba. We had a post office box in Aba for my father's import business. We would spend the third day hurtling south after the line changed over in Kaduna on the second night. Markurdi and River Benue would not be far and then we would feel we were once more in the East. On the morning of the fourth day, we would stop in Enugu for the first large disembarkation of students, heading for Onitsha, Awka and the upper Igbo lands. There was no crying because it was a triumphant homecoming and we knew we would all meet again in three months' time. By midday we would reach Umuahia for another large drop-off of central Igbo lands. The train would now be in wet green lands of the black earth of the Ngwa people of Aba and what a beautiful sight to see after the dry scrub of the north. Rows of cultivated yams on poles and endless forests of palm trees! We were home. Arriving at Aba railway station was like going into a carnival. All our parents were there in their best Sunday dress. It was the day of the return of students from King's and Queen's College, Lagos. Everybody at the Aba Railway station knew about it and so did most of Aba.

We would get out of the coaches, hug our parents and proceed to collect our luggage. I saw my mother in tears of joy, and so was the mother of Benji, my classmate from Aba. Benji and I had not seen much of each other at college. I was very interested in sports and Benji was hopeless at it. Besides, he felt slightly superior to everyone else and had developed a ridiculous posh English accent in which he spoke. He was subsequently known as 'Mersh' because of how he pronounced the word 'much'. Benji went in for theatre and photography, things esoteric even at King's College. We were all back to Aba where we had started but our lives had changed forever. Our clothing was smart and I personally had acquired a pair of brown and white brogue shoes, courtesy of my father who imported shoes like that from the UK. With my long trousers and a bow tie that I had also acquired, I was now a small snob when I went out. At home, my parents realised I had changed considerably. I was taller and my face had filled out, and was no longer like the skinny kid who left six months ago. But perhaps the greatest change, and in some ways the most damaging, was our assurance.

At fourteen we were sure we were superior to everyone else. My father quickly realised the need to find space for me. I had for the first time my own room at the rear end of our house with a window looking into the central patio. This was very useful because I would spend many hours in my room revising my books for the final examinations in December. In the next few days my contemporaries from the local colleges would come to visit and we would stay in my room, drinking 'mineral waters'.

Georgie Spiropoulous from Christ the King College, Onitsha,

would visit, so would Henry Obineche from Government College, Umuahia, Vincent Okoro from St Patrick's College, Calabar, etc. We had all changed and were now separated by our experience and education from our parents and family and from the bulk of the people in Aba. In the evenings during the vacation, we would all go to cinemas together. We even went to photographic studios and had our pictures taken together. We considered ourselves handsome, avant-garde and in a new type of society, well away from that of our parents. The three months' holiday turned out to be rather long and we had to find things to fill our time. I took up learning how to typewrite and spent hours typing on my father's Imperial typewriter using the Pitman's teaching programme. Apart from this, I spent some time helping to sell goods at my father's department store at 33 Asa Road, just as I had done before going up to King's College.

I also visited Port Harcourt where I stayed with my maternal uncle, Joe Onyenakala, who worked as a teacher at one of the schools there. Port Harcourt in those days was a gracious town with nicely planned streets, lots of trees and playgrounds, and was in consequence called the garden city. I did not have any friends in Port Harcourt and I did not know any classmates from Port Harcourt at King's College. I stayed for a couple of days and went back to Aba where I would start a series of holiday correspondence with friends that would run into many pages in later years. This was when I discovered the beauty of the written word – describing in words the sensations and actions one took over the vacation period. It was also a chance to discover who your true friends were. Those who had not replied to your letter were not to be regarded as friends.

The holiday letters from friends came from all over Nigeria, showing how well the postal system worked in those days. But above all, it showed that King's College had succeeded at that time in making us all feel we were all Nigerians and not different ethnic entities. Of course some of the letters from the older students, people a year or two above us at King's College, were surprisingly touching. People talked about missing their friends and revealing the closeness of the relationships. The older students sent what were called 'love letters' to their fags or junior friends, but there was no evidence of homosexuality, to the best of my knowledge. We passed the holiday time as best as we could and waited with trepidation and sadness for the end of September when we would go back to Lagos, this time for a good nine months before we came home again on holidays.

In early September we had already started buying things for the return journey to Lagos. My father gave me a pair of nice brown suede shoes that I would wear for a long time because I could not afford to buy new ones. I had reached my fourteenth birthday that August 1950 in Aba. There was no celebration, just a recognition of my age that day. The trip back to Lagos followed the same routine. We exchanged our government warrants for train tickets at the Aba railway station three days before the journey that was in late September. My mother had increasingly become more and more nervous as the departure date approached. My poor mother had the phenomenal job of cooking several meals (rice, meat stew, fried chicken, fried fish, yam) all in water-less cooking oil in order that the meals would last for four days without growing moulds.

My mother had de-briefed me on the quality of the food she had prepared on my first trip out in January. This time, the oil to be used in cooking would be entirely groundnut oil. Someone had told her that groundnut oil was more heat-resistant than palm oil, and thus you could cook things at much higher temperatures, driving water out and thus preventing mould growth. That was the theory. We would see later on whether she had been right. When the actual day for the return trip arrived, we all went to the railway station early. The tension and sadness was palpable. My father and other relations were stoic. As the train blew its whistle, announcing its arrival into the railway station, my mother broke down in tears. My eyes filled with tears as well. I would once more leave my beloved parents and my beloved Aba and beloved Eastern Nigeria.

King's College and Lagos were now very important features in my life, but leaving my childhood place was always devastating and would remain so for years. So much so that later, over the years, I would dream of taking this train either leaving Aba or arriving in Aba. When the train pulled in with our classmates from Port Harcourt in the reserved compartment, my mood lifted a bit. There were friends from school who I had not seen in three months and I was keen to hear their news. Soon the worry and tears about leaving my father and mother, my brothers and sisters would pass and I would move into a King's College world, even in the train and four days away from Lagos. We got into our respective reserved seats while our proud parents looked on. A few girls heading for Queen's College, Lagos joined the train but we were not really interested. As the train pulled off, I waved goodbye like the other kids to my parents.

My mother was still in tears and I have never forgotten this scene. She loved me and I loved her. I also loved my father and sibling brothers, Emmanuel and John, but I was very attached to my mother. For a good nine years I was the only one she had, after my two brothers and sisters died in the early forties from yellow fever and amoebic dysentery.

Our train left Aba mid-morning, at about 11 a.m., heading as usual for Umuahia, Oturpko and Enugu on the first day. Later the train would cross the Benue River overnight to the north, reaching Kaduna on the night of the second day. We would subsequently head south on the third day, arriving in Lagos on the fourth day. In the train we talked about our holidays. Our reflexes and attitudes as King's and Queen's College students quickly returned. In addition to this my supply of food for the four-day trip was excellent. This new cooking technique used by Mother – everything cooked in groundnut oil – had been justified. There were no moulds on the chicken or meat in my Jerry can after four days. At the Iddo railway station in Lagos, the government PWD truck waited as usual to take us back to the school premises and our dormitories. This familiar routine generated confidence and inoculated us against the panic that is evident in every aspect of Nigerian life today. Once back in the dormitories we regaled friend with our holiday stories. Parents again took a back seat compared with classroom friends.

On our return from the long vacation, a most extraordinary scene ensued at the first school assembly. J R Bunting, the principal, cruised in wearing his black academic gown like a jet airliner coming in to land at an airport. After prayers and school songs, he welcomed all the students and masters back. He then went on to stage an incredible theatrical anger that petrified everyone including staff. In a voice trembling with emotion and sharp blue eyes, he held a newspaper in front of him and read out the following headline, 'Bedbugs at King's College'. There was dead silence. He then went on to say what a disgrace that had brought to the college and that the incident was a scandal that could not be tolerated at King's College!

We did not know how bedbugs had gained access to glorious King's College, but surely it was to be expected someday. The vast majority of students had come from impoverished families who lived in shacks or slums where bedbugs were very common. One or two boys had brought the little beasts back with them from their homes. There followed after that the most major clean-up and disinfecting of the school premises that I ever saw. As September moved on to November, the weather changed to dryer and cooler nights with the advent of the Harmattan winds from the north. December even in Lagos was relatively cold and it was difficult waking up at 6.30 in the morning to go for a cold shower. And still those bells, telling you every hour or half an hour where to be!

Christmas in Lagos

December 1950 would be my first Christmas away from home, away from my family. In addition to that, we would have the promotion examinations to determine who would be promoted to the new class two. The examinations were in early December and the whole school was tense because every class had their examinations. Timetables were posted on a huge notice board. A mixture of determination, ambition and fear of failure propelled me to do well in all my papers. When the results came out in mid December, I had done well and had been promoted to Class 2A! I had not only been promoted but I had moved into the stronger A stream of the school. The first thirty students with the highest marks from the exams were promoted to Class 2A. The rest would be in Class 2B or worse still, thrown out! I was terrified about failing. You must remember that Benji and I were the first kids ever from Aba to enter King's College! King's College was a fair and democratic institution in those days and hard work was duly rewarded. What do you make of a Latin examination at the age of fourteen?

From then on my academic life changed and I was never to look back again. There were rumours that some students had gained entrance into King's College by special concessions, such as that their brothers or fathers had been students in King's College many years earlier. Certainly with the English in charge, the system was not abused. There were a few students from the Lagos area who fell into that category. For country folks who had not even heard of King's College, our only chance to get in was to pass those infernal entrance examinations.

And so these first year examinations were extremely important because it gave the school the first chance to know what type of students they had in their charge. I do not remember any boys being dropped or sent home but in the older classes, it was common to see students who had repeated because some of them joined our class. All that awaited me now was to join in our School Christmas carols and close school for Christmas. School closed with a beautiful ceremony at which we sang Christmas carols that we had spent hours learning in the evenings. The Sunday preceding the end of term, we would be treated to the school Christmas dinner of *jollof* rice and fried chicken and *dodo* in the boarding house. You could buy cold soft drinks if you could afford them. The teachers disappeared from the premises and the local Lagos students plus students from Western Nigeria went home for the Christmas vacation. This vacation would last from the third week of December to the end of the first week in January in 1951. Students from the East, mostly Igbo and Rivers students, had to spend their holidays again on the premises. We could not afford the cost of the train journey back to the East. We had to devise things to keep us occupied over a period of three weeks.

This time, I did feel very lonely – not being with my folks for Christmas and the new year. I remembered how beautifully we had celebrated the season in Aba, with visitors coming to our house all day on Christmas Day. In Lagos, Christmas was celebrated differently. For a start, the department stores were beautifully decorated with buntings and posters of snow and pine trees. I had never seen those before and I was intrigued. I subsequently learnt from a salesman at Kingsway that the Christmas period in England was a cold and dark period with a lot of snow on the ground. The English, he said, cut pine trees and mounted them in front of log fires in their living rooms and decorated them with gifts. Synthetic Christmas pine trees at Kingsway stores were decorated with little plastic stars to remind everyone of the birth of Christ in a manger in Bethlehem. In Aba, at Christ the King Catholic Church, we knew about the manger and little cribs with animals. But these were strictly religious. In Lagos, cribs and the manger were in department stores, with goods advertised at the same time. That was my first contact with the commercialisation of Christmas and I did not like it. Everything was available for sale at Christmas prices.

I had only my three weeks pocket money plus some money I had saved, a grand total of about five shillings. No frivolities here apart from Walls ice cream that I adored. For the rest of the holiday, my friends and I went on excursions to Kuramo Waters and the bar beach on foot. There were no buses to these places in those days. Our excursions usually lasted all day, returning late in the evening to our boarding house. This way, we were able to see parts of Lagos we would never be allowed during term to visit. My favourite places at this time were the creeks at Kuramo Waters or watching the surf break on rocks at the bar beach. In the evenings we would wander across to the marina, near the governor's residence, and watch pleasure boats bring people, mostly Europeans, to and from the governor's residence. Later on, I would learn how to swim during these vacations by visiting the municipal swimming pool at Onikan.

Just about everything we saw in Lagos was new and seemed to reflect a lifestyle in tune with the elite European community. We had access to everything but I knew these things did not exist outside Lagos, let alone in Aba. My taste and lifestyle were being altered in a subtle manner without my noticing. My parents had never seen these things in their life and how would I cope with them when I next returned to Aba? At night, we went to cinemas in a group and that was nice because there was nobody to supervise us. The climax of this vacation would be Christmas Day and of course the new year. The school authorities were very understanding and made arrangements for those left behind in the boarding houses. On Christmas Eve, I went to midnight mass at the Holy Cross cathedral in Lagos. This was quite something. The church was full and mass was celebrated by the Archbishop of Lagos, surrounded by priests. The cathedral was fully lit, both inside and outside. Many people who could not get into the cathedral assisted at the mass from outside. Midnight mass in Lagos was a carnival. There were so many people that vendors selling cold water, ice cream and soft drinks were everywhere. If you had a girlfriend, that was where to be on Christmas Eve. When mass ended at about 1.30 a.m. everybody just strolled around in the cool morning breeze and we would get back to the school compound and wake the gate man to let us in at about 2.30 a.m. The next day we would awake to a special Christmas breakfast of fried eggs and plantain and cocoa. Lunch was also everybody's favourite of jollof rice and fried chicken. But I missed the hurly-burly of Christmas in Aba. Here there were no visitors, no dancers, no feeding of cousins and relations. In a sense we were deprived of a family Christmas, and it would be like that for many years to come. The old family feast of slaughtered goats and chicken was over and I felt I had lost something very precious.

New Year's Eve celebrations in Lagos were also different. In Aba, we all stayed indoors because of the midnight dancers and the throwing of cooking pots and rubbish into the streets to celebrate the arrival of the new year at midnight. In Lagos, the reverse happened. All Lagosians were out in the streets from about 10 p.m. on New Year's Eve. The streets were crowded, creating excellent trading opportunities for food and cold drink vendors. As the time got to near midnight everyone would drift towards the marina where the sea breeze from the Atlantic ocean cooled everyone. The real target was the Anglican cathedral on the marina. Being a Catholic, I was not interested in going in for their religious ceremony, but the bigwigs of Lagos society were always present and it was quite a spectacle watching them going in and sweating in the humid atmosphere.

The other big attraction was the foreign ships in the harbour over the water in Apapa. They rigged up their ships with fairy lights so that the whole of the Lagos seafront had a carnival atmosphere. At the stroke of midnight all the ships would sound their horns celebrating the new year. Many of them would also set off fireworks that I had never seen before. There was a carnival atmosphere and it was fantastic. Young boys with their girlfriends kissed and touched each other up, and we thought it hilarious and naughty and hid to watch. We would lie down on the grass verge by the seafront on the marina till well past 2.00 a.m. and then return to the boarding house. We were within the rules because we had been given permission to be out that night. The big draw was to see who had stayed out the longest. Most of us fell asleep at the marina and went back to college as soon as possible.

These holidays gave me the opportunity to make contact with the students in the year above our class. My class did not have many students who stayed behind in the boarding house at Christmas. In other words, there were not many Igbo boys in Class 2A in 1950.

By contrast the class above me, Class Three, had quite a few Igbo, Rivers, Urhobo and Benin boys who stayed behind in the boarding house because the holiday was too short to travel home to our families. The Class Three boys were worldly, bright, cheeky and mischievous. I was attracted to them and made my best friendships at King's College from that class. They include Gilbert Chigbo, later to become a commissioner in the old Anambra State; Segun Adeyinka, 'Emu' because of his large nostrils; Vincent Maduka, later to become the first African director general of Nigerian Television Authority; Solomon Obi and Daniel Onuogu, successful medical doctors in Nigeria today. I was never really close to my classmates because my friends in the class above had accepted me as their equal. The students in the class above me laughed a lot, made jokes and teased each other mercilessly. I think they were more assured of themselves and the debate still goes on today as to whether that class was cleverer than ours. My own class also had pupils who would later distinguish themselves in various professions. They included people like Lateef Adegbite, now Secretary General of the Supreme Council for Islamic Affairs; Lieutenant General Oluwole Rotimi of the Nigerian Army; Adebayo Ajao, a successful businessman in Lagos; and of course Professor Sowemimo, a distinguished plastic surgeon at the Lagos Medical School.

Leaders from the Playing Field of King's College

The end of the Christmas holiday would be an anticlimax because we had spent some wonderful days by the lagoon in Lagos, visited the mythical bar beach and had stayed out late at night. There was not the slightest fear of being robbed or being beaten up in those days. It was a good period to grow up in Nigeria and in Lagos. School reopened in the second week of January 1951 and we were back to classes as usual. My life in school seemed to progress well because I was soon selected to represent King's College in the junior football competition, which pitted us against Lagos secondary schools, such as St Gregory's College, Igbobi College, Lagos Grammar School and Government College, Ibadan. The King's College junior football team was called the Mosquitoes and nothing was more pleasant than to put on the patchwork jersey of the Mosquitoes for King's College. I played at the outside left-wing position and my job was to pick up balls from an advanced forward position on the left wing and let it fly across to the middle position for the centre forward to ram it into the goal. I must have made some impact because my nickname, Atinkpala, came from my exploits as a rather thin young person flying down the left wing of the football field and whipping the ball across to the centre-forward position for my team-mate to score a goal. This was also the first time that I played football with shoes. In Aba, we played in bare feet and even during my interview at King's College the year before, our test football match was done with bare feet. I was also inducted at this time to train at the nets for cricket.

I was not really good but knew the game well enough to qualify as a reserve for the college first eleven. My problem was that whenever I went under a ball to catch it, it always seemed to bounce out again, hence my other nickname 'rubber hands'. But at least I made the team and represented my school. Later on I would be good enough in athletics and tennis to represent King's

College. Sport was an important part of King's College life, and all-rounders like the Akpata, Nkune and Enahoro families were the uncrowned princes of the campus.

For a start, these families had at least two boys at King's College at any one time. They all excelled in cricket, which was the preferred sport of the principal, J R Bunting; they were very good in football and hockey and excelled again in athletics. The most outstanding sports student in those days was A K Amu who, as a schoolboy, set the Nigerian record for the 440 yards. He set it at the Amateur Athletic Association competition at Onikan police grounds in 1950. He was my athletics hero and he made me his fag in my first year and I was very proud of this. The October to December term was easily the busiest of the year. The weather was more agreeable; the school pitches were nicely green after the heavy rains of July, August, and September, and so there was a lot of sports competitions.

The annual Inter House Athletics Competition was between the four houses of King's College: Hyde Johnson House, Harman House, Mackee-Wright House and Payne House. This was a major school event in which every house presented a team of about 40 students to compete in all the known athletics disciplines of the day. Preceding this was the school's cross-country race over a distance of probably no more than ten kilometres. It was compulsory for everyone in the school to take part. You could only drop out if you had a doctor's certificate. The results of the cross-country race were taken into consideration in the overall points score for the inter-house competition. The course usually went east from King's College gates, then over to the Lagos mainland suburb of Obalende, reaching Ikoyi in places, and in a great arc back to King's College after going round the horse racing track in front of the college. Many Lagos residents would come out to watch as all these youngsters in their house colours of red, green, yellow and blue jerseys would run round looking half dead and doing their school duties. In fairness to the school organisers, everything was in place for people who were either tired or ill or could not complete the race. Selected teachers followed in their cars, or stayed at designated places to pick up those who could not continue. The biggest disgrace was to be seen in a teacher's car being brought back to the premises. You could not live that down.

The inter house competitions were held one week or so after the cross-country race. The inter house competition was probably the biggest event in the school calendar. The college grounds were prepared in advance for the great day with tracks marked on the grounds and pits for the long jump, the high jump and the pole vault dug up appropriately.

This was no small event because the British governor of Nigeria attended these gatherings in a Rolls Royce and the British national anthem and King's College school song rang out across the square. The students who represented King's College in any of the major sports but especially in athletics, were put on special diets of extra meat, fish and worst of all, huge rations of Ovaltine and Horlicks in the evenings. This created an enormous amount of jealousy in those who did not make the grade and could not benefit from the special diet offered to the college sportsmen. But at least the incentive was there. I made the special diet team in my last year of athletics at King's College. The food was special! My objective in class 2A now was to keep my place in the A stream. The opportunity to do so would come in a series of classroom tests that were carried out every week. The weekly tests in Class 2A were used to keep us alert, but also as a means of getting an overall view of our total performance throughout the year and not just at examinations. These were used to give a class assessment and ranking every month. It was hard going because we could no longer go to classes and simply enjoy the lessons. We had to listen carefully and to pass all the exams, some of which were surprise tests.

I did not really mind because somehow my mind clicked in this year and I began to understand my subjects better. And I started getting very good marks that virtually put me in the first five places in the class every month. The reverse side of the medal was not pleasant at all. One or two students in our class wanted to know the others' marks after every test in order to place themselves in the class grid.

They spied on everyone and actually made up their own performance grid across all subjects for the class. It was not nice and people avoided them. Apart from this nuisance, life in Class 2A was exciting enough. For one thing, I met for the first time my contemporaries from Class 1A who I had not talked to when I was in Class 1B. In addition, there were a number of repeat students who had failed their examinations in Class 2 in June and who had to repeat a class. It could not have been very pleasant for them. People who called us fags six months ago were in the same classes with us.

I do not think it really mattered because I became very good friends with one of these repeat students, a friendship which would last for many years after leaving King's College. The other joy of being in Class 2 was that we would no longer be fags because the new recruits in 1951 would take our place at the bottom of the hierarchical ladder. We would have people we would call fags. And so the routine of school life continued pleasantly enough. With time we became more assured and often my classmates and I would get *exeats* to go into town, especially Kingsway to buy ice cream and have instant photographs of us made.

We were allowed one *exeat* per student per month. School rolled on predictably over February, March and April towards Easter. The only thing to remark on was the extremely hot weather preceding the rains that would come around May/June. At the end of this first term of the year, there were examinations as usual with results issued just before the Easter holidays. Once again, those of us from the North and the East of Nigeria would stay behind in the school premises during the Easter holidays while the more fortunate students went home to their families.

A few students from the East had by now found relations living in Lagos. The school allowed these families to look after King's College students as their guardians during the Easter holidays. To qualify as a guardian, an application made by the student's parents would be lodged with the school authorities and approved by them. In effect, once you passed into King's College, the school authorities took full responsibility for your life! The Easter holidays in my second year in 1951 came and went without any significance and we were glad when it was over so that we would again be in contact with friends and resume our student life.

The second term started a week after Easter. We would be going in to the halfway point of the year's syllabus and would be expected to become more and more familiar with our lessons. I coped well with most of the courses including Latin, which most of us learnt off by heart. Imagining us in ancient Rome and speaking Latin was a bit much. By contrast I had great difficulties in two very practical subjects, namely art and woodwork. Apparently, my drawings were invariably flat and, as the arts teacher remarked, I was incapable of getting perspective into my drawings. Perspective is what makes flat drawings on paper look three-dimensional. Worse than my art marks was my woodcraft. A middle-aged Englishman who clearly was from a different family background from our Oxbridge tutors, taught the course. I cannot now remember this teacher's name, but he was kind to the students partly because of his background and nature and partly because no one wanted to do his course. Nobody who had made King's College wanted to end up later in life as a carpenter!

Unfortunately for us, both courses were compulsory for all students up to the end of the third year. The only really nice thing about this hot and stuffy second term was that by the end of June we would be on our way home on the long vacation home to be with our parents and family for three months. We the students from the East had not seen our parents since September of the year before. For a fourteen-year-old, this was not easy; for despite our newly found sophistication, we were still kids and missed our families and our childhood friends. The second term would move quickly and would get to early June when the excitement about the 'long vac' would grip the whole school.

Another Long Vacation

There was a marked relaxation in morning school inspections and in several other departments. But discipline was not allowed to slip. The end of June would see the familiar exodus to western, northern and eastern Nigeria. Igbos from Eastern Nigeria would gather their boxes that had been in storage since last September, wash them out and start packing. Most students would empty their school lockers of clothing and pack their school uniforms into boxes that were safely stored behind. Clothes and shoes for vacation were packed into trunk boxes for the long journey home. Adventurous students bought dark glasses from street hawkers along the marina in Lagos. The excuse was that these glasses helped keep out coal dust from our eyes during the train journey home. Privately we wanted to look glamorous, like American Negro film stars and singers like Nat King Cole or Harry Belafonte, who were our sex symbols at the time. The packing was a joyous period because we were filled with the joy of going home. Lagos after all was big, crowded, noisy and fast. There was nothing more appealing at that time than going back to Aba, to the familiar vegetation of yams, maize, ogede and the black soil of this part of Nigeria. And hearing the Igbo language routinely was reassuring in a way that it is not possible to describe. I was going home. And sure enough, the Public Works Department truck would pull up on the appointed day, pick up our luggage and proceed to have it registered as accompanied baggage at the Iddo railway station for our journey the day after. This worked with great precision for the seven years I was at King's College. I never heard of any lost luggage.

On the day of the journey, we climbed into these government trucks that had no seats and sang our way to the railway station, to travel to our destinations on free government warrants. The journey by train from Lagos through Western Nigeria to Kaduna in the North was followed by the switch of rail tracks in Kaduna to go to Port Harcourt and the East. I have already described this journey earlier. The routine was pretty much the same but it never lost any of its charm or wonder in the seven years I did it. Crossing the River Niger by railway at Jebba was always a wonderful and exhilarating experience. As we rode over the River Niger, I always wondered what would happen if the bridge snapped with our train on top of it. Our journey would proceed placidly through three days and three nights in our special reserved coaches, and in the morning of the fourth day we would stop in Aba to be met by beaming and proud parents. We would get home to our house in some family friend's car or on the back of somebody else's bicycle. I do not remember there being any taxis in those days. It was nice to be home and it was nice to be installed in a special room in our house. My father had decided that as a young man I needed my own room where I could study during the vacation and where I could receive and entertain my friends. It turned out to be an excellent idea. Friends like Georgie Spiropoulous turned up to ask what it was like living in Lagos, the capital of Nigeria and being at King's College. I was very glad to oblige. In August 1951 I was a fifteen-year-old and needed a lot more entertainment to keep me occupied. My old friends and two new King's College students from Aba, Ibegbulam and Strongface would join us to go to the two cinemas in Aba, the Rex and Emy cinemas. We also visited each other in their homes in Aba. This would pale after five to six weeks and I was in search of other adventure to keep me busy.

Luckily my uncle, Chief Mathias Okafor, lived in Onitsha, the biggest market town in Igbo land. This had a special attraction of its own, as a dangerous and sophisticated place. The only Catholic archbishop in Igbo land was the head of the biggest Catholic church in Eastern Nigeria. I wanted to go to Onitsha. My father got word to my uncle and they agreed that I should visit.

This was a marvellous holiday. First, the earth in Onitsha is deep red, the red earth of the Igbo heartland. Secondly, Onitsha people actually regard themselves as the source of Igbo civilisation and spoke a dialect of the Igbo language that was called 'high Igbo'. After all, some of the earliest establishments by the British in Nigeria either for slavery, trade in palm oil, or missionary work, had been in Onitsha. Finally, the foremost Nigeria politician of the period, Dr Nnamdi Azikiwe, came from Onitsha. I visited the main places that were renowned at the time. The Catholic church in Onitsha was so large and impressive I gazed in wonder. But what impressed me most was to go to the edge of the River Niger, at the point where it joined Asaba on the western side of the Niger. The River Niger at Onitsha was now only a few hundred kilometres on its way to the delta and the Atlantic ocean. You could see little boats and large steamboats taking people, lorries and merchandise across the river; people coming back from Lagos and heading for Aba and vice versa. At night, you could see streams of little lanterns put up by people selling smoked freshwater fish caught earlier in the day from the River Niger. Here, you smelt the fresh water of a river that we did not have in land-locked Aba. My meals included a lot of fresh water fish that had a wholesome and refreshing taste.

Besides, my mother was very friendly with the newly married wife of my uncle. She was called Nneka and was actually an Onitsha woman. In those days, Onitsha people did not marry outside of their clan and certainly not a trader from Akokwa. Nneka was as smooth and as polished as you could get in those days and my uncle's rating rose enormously in my estimation. My mother made sure that Nneka looked after me when I was in Onitsha. For many years later I was to be attached to this woman like a surrogate mother.

When my holidays of fourteen days ended in Onitsha I returned to Aba. Even at such an early stage, I noticed that Onitsha was hotter than Aba at night. I did not sleep so well in Onitsha compared with Aba. Also Aba was more cosmopolitan compared with Onitsha. In Onitsha, the vast majority of the inhabitants was overwhelmingly Igbo. There were a few Hausas who lived together in seclusion in their Sabon Gari. This was more to do with their desire to worship in their mosque as Muslims and speak their language, rather than exclusion. In those days, Hausas from the North supplied the cattle and beef eaten in Eastern Nigeria. This interdependence has still not altered today. By contrast the high and low Igbo speakers as well as Efik, Ibibio, Calabari, Yoruba, Hausa and Benin people populated Aba. Even the original owners of Aba, the Ngwa people, regarded themselves as different from the other Igbos. Aba was more varied in its people and this showed at Christmas when the different ethnic groups would put on shows and dances reflecting the varied cultures. I loved Aba for that and was proud to be from there.

On returning to Aba, I did not have much to do either. I had got through the six to eight novels I had borrowed from the school library. One of the books that left a deep impression on me at this tender age was the book by the French aviator and explorer, Antoine de Saint Exupéry. In this book, *Wind, Sand and Stars*, he described in detail what it was like flying over the wide expanse of the Sahara desert. I was literally transported from Aba to the Sahara desert. I have never since read a book that had such an effect on me.

When later, as a university student, I realised that Antoine de Saint Exupéry was a French legend as both an explorer and a writer, I felt very pleased with my early taste in literature. As I did not have any more books to read I persuaded my father to send me to Port Harcourt to spend time with his cousins, the Emeghebo family. People living in Port Harcourt were, by the standards and understanding of those days, more sophisticated than those living in Aba or Onitsha. Port Harcourt was for me only second in importance to Lagos. Port Harcourt was the second maritime port of Nigeria, had an airport and was the headquarters of the Rivers Province. A lot of British officials and businessmen lived in Port Harcourt which was known as the garden city in those days because its streets were lined with trees. Its climate was also more agreeable that the upcountry cities. Even today, Port Harcourt is often 5°C cooler than Lagos at any time of the year. I gladly took the train from Aba to do the 65-kilometre trip to Port Harcourt.

My cousins, including Ignatius Emeghebo, collected me from the railway station and took me to their house in Bende Street in the African quarter of Port Harcourt. Their house was built in the same style as ours in Aba. Yet there was something about their place that appealed to me. There seemed to be a bit more light all around and the streets were definitely cleaner. I think the sanitary inspectors who inspected their houses for stagnant water and rubbish were stricter than their types in Aba. I spent two lovely weeks in Port Harcourt, characterised by eating large quantities of fresh water fish. As an adolescent, I hated fish and I remember vividly my mother insisting I ate all my freshwater fish because it developed the brain. Nutritionists say the same today – talk about old wives tales! I liked dried or smoked fish but did not like fresh fish as a child for three reasons: it had the peculiar fishy smell, which is a mixture of amines and other odours. It is slimy to touch and to taste. It had long bones, which often lodged in my throat and frightened the hell out of me. Many years later, I like nothing more than a nice sole grilled or marinated in butter. I suppose I have educated my taste buds. By the end of August 1951 the long vacation was over and it was time to start buying things for the long journey back to Lagos and another academic year. The return journey to Lagos in September 1951 as a Class 2 student went in pretty well the same manner as the two earlier trips. There were a little fewer tears at the Aba railway station from both students and parents as we were beginning to get used to these annual reunions and departures. It was still sad because we would not see our families for another nine months. However, the effect of all this was to make us into tough, independent little buggers, which was I suppose what boarding schools were set up to do.

The journey over three days and four nights over Nigeria was as fascinating as ever. I did not however like getting back to Lagos and the boarding school. The city strangely was exciting but oppressive. There was a feeling of not belonging! We went back to our dormitories and classes resumed as usual.

Back to School

In this third and final term there would be the end of year examinations for promotion into Class 3A or Class 3B. I settled down quickly after our return and did some serious studying. Apart from a few inter-school junior football matches for the school in the Mosquito Team, I had plenty of time to devote to my studies. The examinations came; I tackled the papers with some calmness. I had to keep my place in the A-stream that I had just achieved a year ago. When the results came out in mid-December I had come out among the top five in my class. I was now certain that moving over into the A-stream a year ago was not a fluke but had been merited.

I often wondered what would have happened if I had not passed that entrance examination in Aba in 1949. I had come into King's College in the last ten students admitted in 1950. With hard work and the right opportunities, I had climbed to the top five two years later. When the Christmas vacation came, those of us from the East stayed behind in the dormitories as usual and made the same excursions to the bar beach, the Onikan swimming pool, the marina for the evening breeze. Strangely enough, I was still not interested in girls. Lagos had a reputation as a wicked city and nobody in his right senses went out with an 'Eko girl'. They were all said to be sexually precocious and would lead us God-fearing eastern boys astray! I still liked going to midnight mass on Christmas Eve at the Holy Cross cathedral, Lagos.

Lessons in Class 3A to which I had been promoted, resumed in the first week of January 1952. One thing that I noticed was that I now fitted better into my school uniforms. I had grown appreciably to fill in the baggy shirts, shorts and trousers my father had made for me when I left Aba in 1950. My father's logic had paid off beautifully. I was more confident in myself and school photographs of those days show a handsome little boy standing in a back row with other students. I no longer had to sit on the grass in the front row as we had done as new students in 1950. The actual lessons in class were infinitely more complicated and serious. In Mathematics, we did algebra and trigonometry. In Chemistry we learnt how to write formulae and balance equations and in history we learnt from beautifully illustrated books about the Ottoman empire, Moldavia and how Turkey, dressed up like a chicken, was the sick man of Europe. As far as I can remember, Nigerian and African histories were not taught except perhaps in the context of the slave trade and its abolition when people like Bishop Ajai Crowder helped to create Sierra Leone for freed slaves from the British colonies.

It has to be remembered that the school's objective was to prepare pupils to take the English University of Cambridge School Certificate (GCE O-levels) and the Higher School Certificate (GCE A-levels). The school curriculum was quite clear on this and in the third year, old copies of school certificate papers of years gone by were circulating in Lagos. You could buy these and thus had a chance to get used to the style in which the exams in the next year would be set. No one student could afford to purchase all the papers and so there was a fair amount of swapping of these papers between friends.

For difficult subjects like Latin, where you were required to translate large sections of Caesar's *Gallic Wars* or the *Aeniad*, your best bet was to buy a complete translation of these masterpieces and learn them off by heart. And that is what most of us did. And so when the tests in class came, what you had to do was to make certain you could translate the first two or three Latin sentences. This would then alert you to what text you were on and all you had to do was just regurgitate the text you had learnt by heart. This worked beautifully until one test in which our teacher, the Ghanaian Mr Winful, deliberately mixed chunks of scripts from different stories into the same translation papers. More than half of our class failed that paper but it showed us the tricks that could be played in examination papers. Being in Class Three meant you were now being prepared for the School Certificate examinations that would take place in less than two years time. For more than half of the class this is where their secondary school education ends, after five years of studies, and they would go out to look for jobs. For the bright ones who would get a grade 1 certificate, they would be invited by the school to stay on for a further two years to do the Higher School Certificate, a prerequisite to university education.

Thus life rolled on like clockwork for the next two years except for a very odd incident that took place in my third year at school in 1952. It was around March in 1952 and the school was getting ready for the annual inter-house sports competition. As usual, the school's playing fields were cleaned up and the running tracks for the 440 yards race and the 100 yards were all meticulously traced out in white on the green grass of the playing field. It was common knowledge that students were not allowed near these fields once decked out.

I was about fifteen years old and had gone to the classroom to collect some books at about 4.30 p.m. On my way back to the dormitory I took a short cut that meant climbing a small fence surrounding the playing field. Someone saw me and immediately told the sports master, Mr S Ade Ojo. The sports master was a corpulent, old and half-blind character who was always in bad humour, probably because nobody ever took him seriously. Mr Ojo bawled out at me and said I had jumped one of the fences and that was a school offence. I tried to explain that I had just crossed a small corner of a little fence and had not meant to flout school rules. Oh no! He had seen me, he claimed, playing hopscotch and jumping over several fences. I was so upset by this manifestly unfair accusation that I burst into tears. Mr Ojo would have none of it and he told me to wait to be called by the principal, Mr J R Bunting, the next day.

Being summoned by the principal was pretty serious because you could be caned and in more severe cases, suspended or expelled from school. Nobody who knew me would have imagined I would flagrantly break school rules. I could not sleep that night. Word had gone round that I was to be seen by the principal the next morning. There were regular culprits who were summoned routinely and caned by the principal. But for me, this was so unfair. My close friends were so upset for me and I got some very good advice from the regulars of school thrashing. I was advised to pack my backside with some exercise books to protect my bottom from the thrashing! The next morning I was in class when Mr Ojo appeared and asked me to proceed to the principal's office.

Of course everybody in class knew why and I felt so humiliated. After all, I was a good student, no 'palavers'. While waiting in the adjoining room, I heard the crash of a cane on somebody's backside. This was repeated three to four times. But I did not hear any scream of pain or sobbing from whoever was being caned and neither was I interested.

When Mr Bunting shouted 'next', it was my turn to go in. He read my offence to me – destroying fences set up for sports day, against the instructions of the school's sports master. Trembling, I protested my innocence and said I had only crossed the end of a fence to take a short cut to the dormitory. He told me that he had to accept the word of the sports master against mine. I was asked to face the map of the world, a reference to a big map on the wall of the principal's office. Mr Bunting was a very tall lanky man and at full stretch, his span was frightening. I got one almighty whack of the cane on my backside, assisted by the notebook I had stuffed underneath my underwear. It was more noise than anything and I had only one stroke! Perhaps Mr Bunting did believe my story, but he had to do something to appease the old sports master. Curiously, this was the first time I was ever to have a one-to-one conversation with the principal. I saw him at close quarters and actually spoke to him. He was an incredibly charismatic man. Later on, friends like Vincent Maduka who became the director general of the Nigerian television authority would say that the man was a gifted actor who modulated his voice and his appearance to impress and frighten people who met him. This probably fits because it was said that Mr Bunting joined the BBC in London after leaving King's College.

Of course the caning meant that my classmates would tease me for weeks about it. The positive side was that at least I had been caned and so had my badge of honour! No longer would my classmates regard me as a wimp or a goody-goody or teacher's pet. Instinctively, I did not expect this caning to be recorded in the school's books against me and it was never raised again. But I was humiliated, especially since I felt I had not committed an offence as serious as Mr Ojo had led the principal to believe. As for old Mr Ojo, the sports master, I kept well away from him. I did not actually dislike him for making me suffer unfairly but I just avoided him for the rest of his stay at King's College. A year or so later he was retired on grounds of old age.

After what had happened, I got a very pleasant surprise when I was chosen from a group of other fifteen-year-olds at school, to write an essay on some aspect of international relations in a competition organised by a United States newspaper (*The New York Herald Tribune*?). The prize was a two-week fully paid trip to Miami in Florida, staying with an American family. There, the successful candidate would meet other fifteen-year-olds from around the world to promote international understanding. When the results of the competition were announced, Benjamin Maduka and myself, the two Aba boys of 1950, were the two selected finalists to represent the whole of Nigeria. It was fantastic but at the same time cruel. Only one of us could go and I so much wanted to win. Of all people, my competitor had to be my mate from Aba! Benji and I were the first two people ever to go to King's College from Aba! Clearly we had made quite an impact at the school. An interview was organised in the principal's office where an American came to talk to us.

We were asked in one at a time, Benji before me. He seemed to stay there for ages and that did not do my confidence any good. Later I was called in and asked all types of questions. If I remember correctly, the objective of the exercise was to get us to engage in conversation rather than see how much we knew. I was not so bold at fifteen. Benji on the other hand, was a self-assured young man who already felt superior to his classmates. Deep under I thought Benji would get it.

I did my best at the interview without feeling overconfident or diffident. All this happened in June and the results would be known sometime in July or August, during the long vacation. The school would send us telegrams in Aba to announce the winner. What a wretched holiday lay before us! We went on our long vacation in July 1952. I tried very hard to forget the test and the reward of two weeks in beautiful, rich Florida with its palm trees and manicured lawns. I was more and more uneasy spending my holidays in Aba mainly because I did not find enough to occupy me during the holidays. I read most of the books I had borrowed from the school library. Every day, I looked out for the elusive telegram. I do not think I told my parents that I was waiting for it. I was afraid of my devastation if I did not succeed. Benji lived just across the Catholic mission compound in Aba, on Asa Road. We had promised each other that whoever won should inform the other; so I could not go to his house to ask him. I did however bump into his elder brother, Young, who knew about the competition and told me they had not seen the famous telegram yet. My long vacation that year was torn to bits with anxiety because the famous telegram did not arrive until August, a good four weeks after we started our vacation.

Benji's elder brother, Young, bicycled to our house to tell me. At that age and in those days, you did not put up a stiff upper lip and say 'Well done' to your rival. I do not remember saying anything. I just crumpled and I think I went to my room to cry. Later I would tell my mother, and not my father, what had happened. My mother, who could not read or write, would tell me not to worry and that it was not that significant going abroad for just two weeks.

Benji would of course be delighted and the local newspaper would carry this news. I was ready to get back to King's College as soon as possible to forget my loss. I was not so unhappy to get back to school in this my third year. My friends at King's College who I missed during the long vacation were beginning to count more than my old friends in Aba did. At the beginning of the third term in 1952, the success of Benji would be announced to the school to great acclaim. I have to admit I wished it had been me. I was a little jealous because the school and the trip sponsors paid for a fabulous wardrobe and boxes to take Benji to Miami Beach. He left Lagos by British Overseas Airways Corporation (BOAC) strato-cruiser to London and from there by Pan American Airways, I think, to New York and then on to Florida. Benji sent me postcards from Miami Beach and of course those royal palm trees and resplendent waterfronts were like nothing we had ever seen in Nigeria. These were places we saw only in films in the cinema. Now one of ours had actually been there and seen them. Benji was to stay with a couple of families in the United States and take part in various youth forums in which he actually represented Nigeria. I would have liked to do that.

In due course Benji came back to King's College and he was required of course to address the school and report his experiences. Well, I can only say that he came across in a very mature and very impressive manner. There and then I knew I could not have achieved what he had. To his honour, he brought back for me a transparent long-sleeved nylon shirt that was in vogue at the time. I was a proud owner of this very elegant see-through shirt. But the trip had changed Benji beyond all recognition. He was more reserved and did not bother with most people. He spoke with an unbelievably posh accent, pronouncing words like 'much' as 'mersh'. This was so ludicrous, that our class and the class above us – Chigbo, Adeyinka, and Maduka – baptised Benji from that day on as 'Mersh'. I am convinced that that trip to the States was to set off a number of incidents in his life, which he could not control, driving him finally into insanity and his early death!

Benji found it difficult to live like the other Class Three students at King's College. He seemed more worldly and restless after coming back from the States. Two years later, he would do his Cambridge School Certificate only and leave soon afterwards for London to a sixth form college to do his Higher School Certificate on his father's funds. In those days, you did not tell anybody if the going was difficult. I think the family could not send him all the money he needed because it was so expensive to study abroad. Four years later, I would arrive in the United Kingdom to study industrial chemistry at the University of Manchester Institute of Technology on a federal government scholarship. Everything was paid for, including our winter clothing.

Benji came to see me at the British Council student's hostel in Lancaster House, Lancaster Gate, just off Bayswater Road in London. Later that year, he would go to Germany where he would have to spend another six months at the Goethe Institute to learn German. After that, he enrolled in Heidelberg, spoke fluent German and made some money by selling Encyclopaedia Britannica to American service families living in army barracks in nearby Mannheim. I kept in touch with Benji and spent my first summer vacation as a university student with him in Heidelberg. I was then twenty-two and a very strong bond grew between us – remember, we had started our journey together from Aba at the age of thirteen. In Germany I was to meet his German and American friends, men and women. A very good-looking boy, German girls were after him. He introduced me to some of his friends and we went to GI parties around Mannheim which did not look very safe. Later Benji would be in some trouble with a German woman doctor who had left her husband for him with a view to subsequent marriage.

This lady would later tell me that she had accepted to be Benji's second wife because Benji had told her that he was already married in Nigeria (which was not true). She was threatening suicide because as she said, she had left her husband and children for Benji and now he would not commit himself. Frankly, I was terrified and thought they might bump Benji off! I had to go to Heidelberg from Manchester. I left Manchester for London by train and then on to Dover from Victoria station in London. I crossed the English Channel by boat from Dover, and took a train from a Belgian port to Heidelberg, to sort things out. I spent a week in Germany and after much discussion with everybody, this German lady absolved Benji of any obligations and let him go. Subsequently, I would lose touch with Benji and never see him again until many years later in Nigeria. Benji would eventually return to Nigeria where I was told he worked for the Nigerian Broadcasting Corporation in the early 1960s; his Oxford accent no doubt finally valorised! But I believe he was already damaged by now, because he had come back without a certificate or degree. He also had little or no money.

I returned to Nigeria in 1965 after my PhD degree in Chemistry from Manchester University and took up a job with the government's Federal Institute of Industrial Research in Oshodi. I lived in Ikeja. Sometime in 1966, I was driving along Ikorodu Road, the main axis between Lagos island and Ikeja and I spotted a well-dressed man with an umbrella and a tie in very dirty clothes. Of course I was intrigued. From how he walked, he looked like Benji. I drove past to get a good look and I thought it was Benji. I was right.

I stopped and called his name and he answered and I asked him if he knew who I was. He said yes. I asked him to climb into my Renault Caravel, a sports car I had just bought, second-hand, from a French man who worked for Renault in Lagos. Benji was already down on his luck and probably not far from going mad. I took him home to my residence at the GRA Ikeja. He had not eaten for some time and it was clear his clothes had not been washed for more than a week. I gave him some clothing of mine while his clothes were taken from him and washed and ironed. He stayed overnight, had a good bath and slept well. We had a good meal together at which he did not say much and never told me what he did or where he lived. He said he wanted to be back in Lagos and so on the second day, I drove him back to Lagos. That was in late 1965 and that was the last time I saw Benji, my dear friend from Aba.

On January 15, 1966, the first military coup d'état in Nigeria occurred. The Biafran civil war started soon afterwards and the Igbos were being hunted down in the North. I left Nigeria on the same day for a research fellowship at Sussex University in the UK. After the war, in 1970, I came back to Aba, near the centre of the final onslaught on Biafra, to see what had happened to my family. I also asked about Benji and my youngest brother told me that Benji was the principal announcer and main voice of Biafra Radio during the civil war. Everybody in the East knew the voice of Benjamin Maduka, with his polished English accent, but nobody ever saw him. He was moved around with the radio station to avoid capture or aircraft bomb. They finally got him because I understand that he died during the Biafra civil war of 1967 to 1970. He would have been no more than 33 years old. That visit to the USA at the age of sixteen changed Benji and he paid a heavy price for it.

The rest of 1952 and 1953 moved fairly fast. In 1953 I was in class 4A, the final year before the Cambridge Overseas School Certificate, the equivalent of the GCE O-level. In Class Four you had to choose the subjects you would offer for examination in the next year, Class Five. I chose nine subjects: English, English Literature, Latin, History, Geography, Maths, Physics, Chemistry and Biology. We had to work hard because the school's reputation depended on the results. The Cambridge University examination board in the United Kingdom set the papers and the chances of fraud were negligible. Our teachers drilled us by setting surprise examinations from old examination papers. You had to do well in Class Four to be allowed to go into Class Five and the School Certificate examination. In Nigeria in the 1950s, this was an important certificate to have. Many Nigerians did not possess it and getting it was an overwhelming ambition because it was the lowest rung on the education ladder.

No Sex – We are King's College Boys

I was nearly seventeen when I first took any real interest in girls. It was in 1953. The little adolescent crushes I had in Aba at eleven were really not serious. At King's College, rumour had it that some of my classmate like A K Bello and O Popoola, a classmate of Chigbo's, were so 'old' that they already had wives before they came to King's College. Of course that was impossible, but we preferred to believe it. What was evident was that a few of these fellows were sexually precocious. They almost certainly were no longer virgins and had had sexual relationships before. Those of us who were still virgins had a terrible time. I think most of the fellows from the East probably were. There we were in Lagos, in an all-boys school, cooped up together for nine months of the year. We did not know how to approach girls and at seventeen this was slightly pathetic. The number of boys in my year that had wet dreams every night can only be imagined. Every morning, our bed sheets were spotted with the results of our previous night's efforts. We went round looking at people's bed sheets and told everyone else who had drawn the biggest 'map of the world' the night before. If you had wet your bed, you covered it up pretty quickly. We did not masturbate because we did not know about it. The local daytime boys, mostly Lagos residents, had girlfriends from the local girls' schools such as Ahmaddiya Girls High School or Lagos Grammar School or Methodist Girls High School. These were day schools and each girl went home after the day's classes.

As King's College students and boarders and non-Yoruba speakers, most of us from the East did not stand any chance with Lagos girls. And yet they were the only girls available. And so sometime in 1953 when I was in Class 4A, I was in the town centre on *exeat* to buy some school equipment. I was dressed in the now famous all-white school uniform of King's College, complete with school badge and tie. I was at the CMS (Church

Missionary Society) bookshop in Broad Street and noticed a rather pretty young girl, no more than sixteen or seventeen years old. She did not have the typical precocious look of Lagos girls, who were reputed to have early sexual experience. I followed her around the bookshop and finally picked up courage to ask some stupid questions. She turned round to look at me and she and her friend burst out giggling. I blushed like hell and if I had been a European my face would have been a deep purple! I was sure everybody in the bookshop was watching me, and I just wanted a hole into which I could disappear. I left the bookshop and waited at the entrance for Bimbola, I think that was her name, and her friend to come out. I think they were a bit scared to see me still around. But then, my badge, a King's College boy, was not to be spat at. I stuck with the two girls and walked with them for quite a while. They lived in one of the back streets behind King's College and so I could in fact walk most of the way with them. I do not remember going on any buses. It was very hot and humid, as Lagos is most of the time. I tried to make a conversation in my Oxford English which we learnt at King's College. The two girls replied in monosyllables but most of the time spoke to each other in Yoruba. I think they had seen King's College students before and when it came to chasing girls especially Lagos girls, we were a joke.

I managed to get Bimbola's name and knew where she lived because I followed her home. I tried to make a date for two week's ahead and she readily agreed that we would meet again at the CMS bookshop, mid-afternoon two weeks on. I came back to the boarding house with my head in a spin. I actually had made contact with a girl. I had a Lagos girlfriend! I reported my good luck to a close friend – I cannot remember whom, probably Chigbo. He laughed and told me I did not stand a chance. He was certain the girl already had a Lagos boyfriend, a 'local thug' with whom she had sexual relationships on hot Lagos nights. Bimbola, he said, had agreed to see me in two weeks' time simply to get rid of my 'English grammar' and me. I was devastated. And later, events would show that Chigbo was right. I went back to the CMS bookshop two weeks later to meet Bimbola after her day's school. Needless to say, she was not there. I recognised her friend and asked what had become of Bimbola. It finally became clear she was rather terrified at meeting me again and had ducked out of our meeting. Meeting me was more like being with a foreigner – a European – rather than being with a Nigerian. I did not speak Yoruba and she was not that sure of her English. Besides, it was almost certain that she had a local schoolboy probably from Lagos Grammar School whom she saw every night when they roamed the streets to buy some suya or dodo and snuggled together afterwards. Of course I was deeply disappointed. To my friends, it was a big joke and for the Igbo boys at King's College, it was foolhardy of me to go for a Lagos girl who hardly spoke English, since I did not speak Yoruba.

And yet, much later in the 1960s, there were to be deep emotional relationships, often resulting in marriages especially among Nigerian intellectuals in universities, between the Igbos, the Yorubas, the Hausas, the Efiks and Rivers people. Each found something they could not get from their own ethnic grouping! I did not give up my pursuit and the initial rebuff made me more determined.

I decided to take lessons from my older colleagues, on how to woo this girl, and what to say if I ever saw Bimbola again. One or two of my Yoruba day-student friends knew this mysterious girl and agreed to help me locate her. I was delighted. But that should have rung a bell, because if my friends knew this girl then she was obviously notorious and I would be no match for her. Bimbo was duly located and through intermediaries I would arrange to meet her again on one of her walks home from school. She covered the two kilometres from around Tinubu Square in the centre of Lagos to her home in one of those peculiar old Brazilian houses in the slums of Lagos, off Igbosere Road, on foot. When I recognised her in the company of two other girls, I called out and she turned and saw me. I think she was embarrassed because I needed to talk to her without her girlfriends listening in. She asked her friends in Yoruba to drop off, which they did. They were just a few metres behind, gossiping. When I got my chance with Bimbola, I started off by literally reciting the wooing speeches I had learnt from friends at King's College. She listened but I think probably wondered what nut she had met. Her English was not very good and it is doubtful if she understood all that I was saying. She did know though that I was fond of her, because she allowed me to accompany her in my school uniform all the way to within a few metres from her home when she asked me to leave her.

It was not exactly good for her image to be seen with a King's College boy. Her friends would tease the hell out of her for being a snob and going out with a King's College boy. Her boyfriend would probably beat the hell out her. We met this way for several months, after which she finally agreed to visit me at King's College on one of those famous Sunday evenings. For me this was a great coupe because I could dress up on a Sunday and show my contemporaries that I had a girlfriend in Lagos.

My friends knew of Bimbola's visit to King's College the moment I started dressing up after siesta on this fateful Sunday afternoon. Everybody who dressed up on a Sunday attracted attention because they had visitors coming: their parents and relations or a girlfriend. If you were from the East, your visitor was unlikely to be your family because they were 600 kilometres away. And so, I, an Igbo, was to be visited by a girlfriend and everybody wanted to know 'the quality of the meat'. As visitors' hour approached, I moved towards the main gate of the school premises where visitors came through. She did arrive and was shown to the visitors' room where I joined her. I cannot now remember, but I think the school provided orange squash and biscuits that we could offer to visitors. Bimbola looked a perfect guest, nicely dressed and pretty in that rakish Lagos way. I tried to make conversation but it was hard going. It was worse than receiving a visitor in prison. Visitors and students all sat together in the visitors' room and there was certainly no chance of sneaking away for quick snog in a corner. I was very proud though of having received a girlfriend even if I had not got anywhere. I made sure my classmates saw us together which was probably a mistake.

For when all the visitors had left three or four of my friends surrounded me. The Lagos boys among my friends promptly told me they knew who Bimbola was. According to them, she was not the innocent little girl who had come to visit me but an experienced raver in the back streets of Obalende, a suburb of Lagos. Of course I refused to believe them, accusing them of jealousy.

But the doubts had set in. From now on everyone would tell me where they had last seen her in Lagos and who she was with. That was not nice at all and I finally threw in the towel. I was not to make any serious moves towards having girlfriends for another two years until I got into the lower sixth. The rest of the school year went well, with one term following another agreeably enough. At the end of 1953 we had our examinations and most of us were promoted to Class 5A. A few students deemed unsuitable for the school certificate examinations were not promoted. These students came from wealthy parents and they were promptly sent abroad to the United Kingdom where they would enrol in specialist colleges for the GCE O-level.

Preparing for the 'School Certificate'

The Cambridge Overseas School Certificate was known for short as the School Cert. This was the single most important certificate in education that you could have in the colonies. It was the equivalent in those days to the GCE O-level. The year 1954 saw those of us lucky enough and bright enough, promoted to Class 5. For this new class, things would prove very tough and rough. At the end of the year, we would do the School Certificate examinations. The certificates awarded after the examinations would be the first internationally recognised certificates we would get. For some, this was their last year at school and their School Leaving Certificates would accompany their Cambridge Overseas School certificates. In addition to these, schools in Nigeria were ranked by the quality of the results they obtained in the School Certificate and Higher School Certificate examination.

It was the turn of my class year to show how bright King's College boys were. This was no easy task because the class of the year above us, the classmates of Chigbo, Adeyinka, Onuogu and Maduka, had the year before obtained apparently the best School Certificate results King's College had ever seen. In addition to this, the results of the School Certificate examinations would also be used to stream us into science and arts classes for the sixth form and subsequent Higher School Certificate examinations.

It was as if all our lessons up till now had been rehearsals for the real thing. We took our classes seriously in 1954 and when the examinations arrived in November, the northerly Harmattan winds were already blowing. The grass on the school lawn was dry, the mornings were cold, dry and hazy, adding to the strange atmosphere in the school. At night, those of us in the fifth form were preparing for the School Certificate examinations. Senior students in the upper sixth class who were in their seventh year were also preparing for their Higher School Certificate.

Everyone else had internal school examinations for their

annual promotion. The atmosphere throughout the school was tense and the most popular commodity on the school premises was 'kola nut'. This is a locally grown fruit that is either white or red in colour, has a bitter taste and has a reputation for keeping people awake, like caffeine in coffee. It is a stimulant and extracts are said to be present in Coca-Cola. We sent day students to buy special types of kola nuts for us. We ate them at around midnight when one of us doing the exams would be designated to wake up the others. This would keep us awake at night up to about 4.00 a.m. when we would go back to sleep. For four hours, kept awake by kola nuts, five or six students would congregate by corridor lamps because the main lights of the dormitories were switched off. The class above mine was even more desperate. They drank black coffee, immersed their feet in bowls of cold water or wrapped their heads in cold towels while others slept over their books. One daredevil reputedly got caffeine powder from his elder brother who was then at the University of Ibadan and sold it to his colleagues who wanted to stay awake all night. Drug peddling at King's! He assures me he never took it himself.

We will never know whether swotting by corridor lights helped us, instead of getting full nights' sleep, but it helped our confidence because we could say to each other that we had been up all night revising our texts. What I remember clearly from this period was learning by heart large chunks of the English translations of the Latin text of Caesar's *Gallic Wars*. By sheer chance it paid off, because in the Latin paper, some of the Latin text of the *Gallic Wars* came up as a major piece for translation into English. In addition to Latin, we had eight other papers to cope with such as English Language, English Literature, History, Geography, Maths, Physics, Chemistry and Biology. The examinations for the School Certificate and Higher School Certificate were held in the large school assembly hall and it was quite intimidating.

At the end of each paper, you met with friends who helped your morale by telling you that they also had found the papers difficult. There were then the class spies who let you know that the papers were so easy they had finished ten minutes before time was up. That left me wretched because I never finished any paper before the time was up. Only the final results would tell whether they were bluffing. The School Certificate and the Higher School Certificate examination papers for the whole of Nigeria were sent back to England for marking. The results were sent back to Nigeria through the Ministry of Education and then sent on to the various schools. We got ours at King's College around the third week of December, and certainly before school closed. It was posted on the main school notice board.

As soon as it was up, word got round and people converged at the main board which hung on the first landing of the Tudor-style administration building. A few teachers came out from the staff room when they heard students screaming. I had scored four Cs and five As! The Cs were in the arts subjects – English, Latin and Geography. By contrast I had As in all the science subjects: Maths, Biology, Chemistry, Physics and also in History. Our Chemistry teacher, Mr Thomas, was walking up the stairs at this moment to the staff room. Mr Thomas walked slowly with a swivel in his right leg because he had been wounded during the last war.

He saw me, beamed a wide smile and congratulated me. I had passed my School Certificate in Grade One! That was something to celebrate. I do not now remember if I did anything like celebrating, not having too much money. All that I remember is that I was extremely happy and promptly wrote my father and mother in Aba to pass on the good news. This was the first tangible result for the six years of sacrifice they had made for me and I had not disappointed them.

Christmas in 1954 was very welcome and we waited for the annual Christmas dinner in school. Students from the East, as usual, stayed behind in the dormitories. We did not do so with any joy because, whatever else was said, we were not celebrating Christmas with our families. In 1954, I missed not celebrating Christmas with my family very much. After all I had just made a Grade One in the Cambridge School Certificate, and I couldn't see my family to tell them personally. Some students, who had not done so well or had failed, were asked to leave the school. That was the end of their path at King's College and it was sad.

Others from wealthy parents were promptly put on the Elder Dempster Shipping Lines and sent to England to special finishing schools to repeat their School Certificate examinations and secure good grades to go into sixth form colleges in England. Those of us who were bright but did not have wealthy parents did not have a chance to travel overseas for further education. I think we were envious because in those days, among the more senior students, the talk was about who was sailing to the United Kingdom for further studies. One or two of my friends from the fifth form left this way. That brought home to me how poor some of us were! Still, life had to go on and in the next year, 1955, we would be in the sixth form, an important and very formative year for all of us. When school reopened after the Christmas vacation, the composition of our class would change dramatically. First we were now split into two classes – the arts and science sixth form classes. The second major change was that we had now to chose subjects which we would specialise in with a view to going on to universities. This meant choosing careers, and that was quite difficult if you were eighteen years old and in Africa. Who were your role models in pre-independence Nigeria, whose careers you would like to follow? Frankly they did not exist.

I had vague ideas of being an agricultural engineer or a medical doctor, as my father wanted. Either way, I was in science and so I chose to do four science subjects for the Higher School Certificate in two years time: Physics, Chemistry, Botany and Zoology. English was compulsory for everyone. Our teachers were wonderful mentors who had been with us for the past year since our School Certificate Examinations.

In Physics we had the stocky Nigerian teacher who was responsible for the school's Photographic Society, Mr Ibi Mboto, a brilliant teacher who was both hard and mean with money. Mr Bestman, the impeccably dressed Physics master for the school certificate, had been dropped. Another young, good-looking Nigerian graduate from Anambra taught botany, Mr R C Onyejepu. He was also impeccably dressed and spoke with a lisp. One of the expatriate teachers' wives had a crush on him. For Zoology, we had the youthful John Marcroft who was by now a friend.

The Welshman, W G Thomas, taught my favourite subject, Chemistry. The science stream had some good students like

Binitie and Emodi but the outstanding ones included people like Sowemimo, Boboye and Akindele from Lagos Grammar School. The others went into the Arts sixth-form class. The third devastating change that occurred in this sixth form was that some girls were going to join us as day students! We had seen some girls in the sixth forms in the years before us but they were our seniors and really made no impression. Two Calabar girls, Etuk and her friend Udoaffia, several years earlier, had created a lot of havoc on sports day when these girls had to run or jump. They could do neither, but the sight of girls' breasts heaving up and down in an all-male school was more than we, as juniors, could take. Most of the girls in Etuk's group were plain, studious and wore glasses. But Etuk and her pulpous friend, Udoaffia, were beautiful and adorable. They did create problems at school because there were often disputes between senior students that could be traced back to their male classmates seeking their favours. After all, in that sixth form in 1953, there were just five girls in a class of 30.

In our lower sixth form class of 1955, we had about seven girls, all day students, who had been recruited from Queen's College and Methodist Girls School. Before long these girls would make their liaisons with their favoured choices among the boys. There was a continuous changing of relationships as the girls found better friendships with time. We also had four or so male students who had come in from other schools in Lagos where the Higher School Certificate course was not offered. The most famous of these students was Akindele, who had come in from Lagos Grammar School. He was subsequently to qualify as a medical doctor from the University of Ibadan and be an out-standing doctor in Lagos. As a new student, Akindele was outrageous. He was the loudest in the class and knew all there was to know about Lagos life. Soon it became obvious that if you were not his friend or crony, your life would be hell. A reasonable student, he was average in sport, but you would not think so from how he talked. Akindele would briefly be my mentor, helping me get closer to one of the girls in our class who I shall call here Miss Idris. I was crazy about her. She was small and not particularly pretty. I suppose I never saw any of that. Miss Idris briefly became my girlfriend in a very platonic way. She was much more mature emotionally than I was and probably a year older. Akindele was to open my eyes by telling me that she probably had a boyfriend in town. He was right because these girls went home from school every day to houses and lives in town that were very removed from the refined collegiate atmosphere of King's College. A subsequent principal of King's College, Augustine Ibegbulam, who superseded us as student from Aba, recently told me that I used to pass messages to Miss Idris through him and that I had used him as my messenger!

In addition to introducing girls into our class, a number of my classmates had been appointed school prefects; people like Rotimi and Ibeziako. The school captain was from the class above us and I was glad to know that none of the senior students I fraternised with was a school prefect – Chigbo, Maduka and Adeyinka were too irreverent, called people names and laughed at teachers and were unfit to be made school prefects! I think one or two of them made it to house prefects. By contrast Onuogu, quintessentially bookish and serious, was made school prefect. Akpoyoware was made school captain.

The school captain had one important privilege – he had a room to himself. One captain who subsequently played an important role in Nigerian society shut himself in with a girl on visiting Sunday, for hours. Of course, word got round of what had happened and a group of students waited by the school captain's room for the door to open. The captain and his girl-friend came out later, totally exhausted while a twitter went round the ground. Nobody thought they had been drinking orange squash all afternoon!

Some of the earlier prefects were legendary for their rigour and were described as 'wicked'. I remember Philip Asiodu who was a prefect in my second year at King's coming round to inspect our dormitory after cleaning. He bent over and stroked the polished wooden floor with his fingers and of course picked up some dust. He asked the poor student who had cleaned the floor to polish it over again. Kalader Hart, 'Old man Hart' from Port Harcourt, also a prefect, was also considered 'wicked'. He used to abandon whatever duties he was on, every night, at a few minutes to junior lights out and sprint to the dormitories, repeating to himself, 'I am going to punish any boys late for lights out'. It was said that his shirt pocket was stained because of the frequency with which he dipped his hand into it to get out his notebook and pen to record punishments.

What Was Your Name?

No story of King's College would be complete without mentioning the nicknames that made us all equal – from school master to captain to first year fags. The only people who did not have nicknames were the boring, creepy students or masters. Students invented names by observing some odd behaviour pattern, mannerism or look of a fellow student. The names were often cruel and they stuck with you for the rest of your lifetime. Here are a few examples:

Atinkpala	– Ibekwe:	a thin-legged gazelle in the Yoruba language, because my legs were so long and thin
Agbon	– Unachukwu:	coconut in the Yoruba language because his head was shaped like a coconut
Aggresso	– Flanagan:	our Irish-born English teacher with a fiery temper
Bedlam	– Aboluwole:	nobody knows why he was called that name
Dodo	– Ademakinwa:	fried plantain/bananas. A day student who came to classes with dodo in his pocket as his day snack. His pockets were always stained yellow from cooking oil
Eba	– Adedipe:	pounded manioc. A teacher caught him day-dreaming in class just before the end of school and told the class that the fellow was already thinking of lunch, which that afternoon was Eba

Imu	– Adeyinka:	nose in the Yoruba language because he has large nostrils
India	– Dan:	he specialised in buying cheap Indian booklets that promised short cuts to everything, from love letters to passing examinations
Medusa	– Maduka:	from mythology; it rhymed with his name; others said he looked like one. Had they seen a Medusa?
Omega	– Adeyemi:	for the Greek letter W. This fellow was called 'Double Omega' or 'Walking Wickedness', because he showed no mercy in how he doled out punishments as a prefect
Palita	– Thomas:	Welsh Chemistry master who spoke with a broad Welsh accent and could not say 'per litre' without a sing-song tone
Pongo	– Obi	baby gorilla
Scrape	– Onabolu:	he was always in trouble with the prefects
Skull	– Unachukwu:	he had a bony face and a massive toothy grin
Tuba	– Okafor	root crops like yam or manioc are called Tubers. He was massively built and consumed large quantities of tubers at school
Wamba	– Chigbo:	Shakespearean court jester. He was the class clown and called people names
Wee	– Akpoyoware:	short for wisdom – smart and tricky

Footsteps in the Sand

In 1955, I was in the lower sixth class, just one year before leaving King's College forever. If I was to be remembered, this would be the year when I would have to do something memorable. I threw myself with enthusiasm into just about all school activities. It was also the year when all my sports potential would manifest. I was now eighteen-plus, still a lanky child, but had filled in nicely to be selected to represent my house, Harman House and King's College in cricket, football, tennis and athletics. During the year, I won the long jump event in the inter-house competition, with a leap of 20 ft, 10 inches. For this, I received a trophy from the wife of the governor of Nigeria, Sir John Macpherson. That tells you how close to the seats of power King's College was. I did reasonably well in sports but was not one of the stars. We were jealous of the sporting heroes. In cricket and football, I was more often than not in the reserves, because there were outstanding players like Sonny Akpata in cricket and Ibeziako in football. But in tennis and athletics I was in the school team proper.

In addition to these I was involved with several other societies like King's College Society – a debating club, Straw Club, the Red Cross, etc. 1955 was easily the busiest year of my stay at King's College. As young people in a prestigious institution we felt that the future was ours. Nigeria at this time had an elected chamber of politicians in the House of Representatives. These politicians represented the three main regions of Nigeria, namely the North, the West and the East. We were encouraged at King's College to learn about democracy and government because each class had civics lessons where we learnt about the United Nations and governance. The school got tickets enabling us to visit the House of Representatives to see our politicians at work. It was very impressive to watch Parliament in session. We saw the Western politicians led by Chief Awolowo. Sir Ahmadu Bello led the northern politicians and Dr Nnamdi Azikiwe nominally led the

East although he had actually been elected in Yaba. In those days, as young adolescents, we were able to see at first-hand the malaise that would eventually lead to a civil war.

Each ethnic group emphasised their origin by their manner of dress and gestures. Representatives from Western Nigeria wore grandiose *Agbada* dresses. Eastern politicians like Barrister Jaja Wachukwu and Barrister Raymond Njoku from Aba were dressed in European suits with Homburg hats while others especially from the Rivers Province wore long tunic shirts. Some of the other Igbo politicians distinguished themselves by wearing long red tunic shirts with red Muslim-type hats topped with a white bird feather. Not surprisingly, I identified with them and with Dr Nnamdi Azikiwe especially. Northern politicians led by Sir Ahmadu Bello and his deputy, Tafawa Balewa were majestic in their turbans. You could only see part of their faces because most of them were wrapped up in huge turbans. Balewa's voice was magnificent with the purest Oxford accent when he spoke.

We saw a number of the more elderly representatives asleep in the comfortable air-conditioned chambers. The newspapers would later report these things in very unflattering terms, ridiculing the politicians, mostly from the North. This would lay the foundation for the deep divide and distrust between Northern and Southern Nigeria. No one had the right to ridicule the Northerners at that stage because their system of government had up till then been based on indirect rule, with the British handing over power to the emirs, who then told the ordinary people what they wanted them to do. The whole representative system of government was new, as new and as strange as people like me being at King's College.

At that period in time, things did not seem so bad for us at King's College; we saw it as our duty to take over the government when independence came. We would give as good an administration as the British had given us. After all, King's College had been set up precisely to produce future leaders of Nigeria in much the same way as Eton or Winchester schools in England had produced their leaders. This was a good time to be a teenager in Nigeria and we were full of hope – hope that was encouraged in no small measure by our expatriate English teachers who made us feel we could do anything.

It was also precisely at this period that two West Indian Olympic gold medallist in the 440 and 220 metres races, Arthur Wint and Macdonald Bailey, were invited to Nigeria after the Olympic Games to demonstrate their skills. Our principal, J R Bunting who had been the principal in a government college in Jamaica, knew them and invited them to King's College to talk to us. The two gentlemen were so handsome and svelte that we were not surprised they were champions. Wint and Bailey quickly became known as 'Wheat and Barley' to the wags at King's. All in all, my sixth year at King's College would be very busy and satisfying.

I do not remember much about the annual long vacation but I do know that some time that year I was to meet a lady, five years older than myself who would be the first woman I would fall in love with. I shall call her Rachel in this account. She was a teacher at the kindergarten class of the Holy Cross Catholic school, Lagos. I do not remember how I first met her but I think it was after Sunday mass at the Holy Cross cathedral in early 1955. She had led in a group of kids for mass and I had arrived with King's College Catholics, just as the children's mass ended. We must have exchanged pleasantries as she led her kids out of their chairs and I installed our boys in their seats. She was so mature and very beautiful compared with our scrawny, brainy sixth form girls at King's College.

It is all very vague now, but I must have asked to see her again the next Sunday after mass. She said yes and the next Sunday she was waiting for me before we arrived. That was the first time a girl had not given me the run-around. She was Yoruba but played this down and spoke to me in fluent English. She told me a bit more about her work as a schoolteacher at Holy Cross school and about where she lived. She confided in me that she walked to school every morning passing King's College by the race course road at about 7.30 a.m. Luckily for me as a senior student, my dormitory was in the new wing, opposite the racecourse. And so for the next few weeks, from Monday to Friday, I would stand by the corridor of my dormitory to wave her off to school. She would turn round and wave back to me with a smile but without saying a word. She always wore a dress in white or pale colours, rounded off with white high-heeled shoes. I could not believe my luck and I began to believe that perhaps I really had something special. Finished were the illiterate skirmishes with Bimbola.

As for my Miss Idris of the sixth form, I lost all interest and it showed. My classmates got wind that something was up because students in lower sixth collected letters for students every morning. It became obvious that I was receiving three to four letters every week in blue or purple envelopes, in a carefully written hand. Rachel wrote to me every other day to tell me how she felt the day before when I had waved her goodbye to school. A few 'bad' boys in my class, especially Adegbite, today a prominent lawyer and secretary general of the Muslim League of Nigeria, announced to my classmates that he thought I had a new girlfriend because I received a letter every other day with a Lagos postmark!

Word got round in the sixth form that this lady and Sam Ibekwe waved to each other every morning at 7.30 a.m. at a given point. The next morning a few of the bastards pretended to be busy on this corridor and at exactly 7.30 when dear Rachel turned to wave to me, four or five boys stood next to me to howl 'they are in love'. I wanted a hole to disappear into. If this were to continue, I said to myself, I would lose Rachel. That Sunday after mass I discussed the orchestrated cheering with her and calmly she told me not to worry because she did not care either. I think she was probably in love with me as well. This relationship became the most important thing in my life at this stage.

Sometime that year, King's College dramatic society put on a play by T S Elliot, *Murder in the Cathedral*. It had a mixed cast of teachers, their wives and students. The expatriate wives made our clothes for the play. The English wife of one of the teachers, Mrs Manley, was one of the nuns and also made some of the clothes. John Marcroft, the handsome bachelor Zoology teacher, was one of the knights. Mrs Manley made his knight clothes and brought them in one evening for dress rehearsals. She was all over Marcroft who blushed so strongly that his whole body, not just his face, turned red. Mrs Manley seemed pretty besotted with the boyish Marcroft, with his long blond hair. Marcroft's voice cracked during the rehearsals and everyone looked at each other since Mr Manley was present, directing the play with Agresso the

Irishman. Gilbert Chigbo, Akpoyoware, Adegbite and myself were in the play. I was one of the priests at the altar when the archbishop was murdered. Each player in the cast was given two free tickets to invite friends or relations from outside the school. It was a big thing because senior European and Nigerian officials attended and I think the governor of Nigeria came one evening.

It was really impressive because the school got all the necessary lighting and music put together and the main school hall was converted into a theatre. The stands and castles were all designed and painted by school staff. I had my two tickets and since I had no relations in Lagos, I could not invite anybody. That was, until I saw Rachel the next Sunday and told her about the play. She said she would come on the third and final night of the play. I gave her the ticket and waited in fear to see if she would turn up. On that day, we put on the play as usual and there was no way I could look into that audience of 600 or more people to see if she had come. I slugged on until the final curtain. We bowed to tremendous applause. As I was taking off my black cassock, a soft voice called out to me in the dressing room. Rachel had come personally behind the curtains to congratulate me. She had not only sat through the play but she had come backstage to congratulate me. I was over the moon. I was now certain that she cared for me.

The fact that she was at least five years older than me was even more comforting. She was not going to be another young thing playing at being in love. For the next six months I waved to Rachel from the balcony of King's College nearly every morning at about 7.30 a.m.

If I missed out for one reason or another, I got a letter two days later asking if I was all right. I waited for Sunday morning mass where I would have the chance to talk to her. In the evening on Sundays, she visited me at King's College. I was overwhelmed with happiness and my classmates knew it.

The teasing was incessant. I finally knew what being in love meant. In early 1955, I was made a house prefect, a position of some authority but below that of a school prefect. My friends in the class above, Chigbo, Maduka, Onuogu, Adeyinka were getting ready for their Higher School Certificate examinations. More than any other year, students in that class were my role models and I watched carefully how they performed. They were serious and, by and large, irreverent and bright. At the end of the year they would be gone and my year would take on the mantle of seniority. This sense of responsibility would influence whatever I did in the last twelve months of my life at King's College. I had come in as a waif in 1950 and six years later in 1955 I would be doing my bit to defend the institutions of the school. I think I was a popular senior student and made quite a number of friends in the junior classes, friendships that last up till today.

This sense of responsibility made me react fairly severely to a growing relationship between Patrick (Paddy) Ekpunobi, a good friend and classmate, and one of the new girls in the sixth form from Queen's College. This young lady was undeniably attractive but also pushy. There were rumours that she and Paddy had been seen making love at the back of the school stage.

This was a bad example to the junior school who started the gossip, and as a house prefect in Harman House to which Paddy belonged, I tackled Paddy about this and of course he said there was no truth to the story. Another student from the class below mine, an Aba student of all people, was also said to be 'knocking off' this girl. I was scandalised, because you could do whatever you liked outside King's College, but not within the premises. I had no proof of these allegations and therefore I could not report the incident to the school captain or to the school principal. This sort of behaviour could not be tolerated on school premises, as it would give the younger students the wrong signal. Besides, everyone was talking about it. I think I was probably a tinge jealous of their guts. But it was not on and could not be tolerated. And so one afternoon, while the majority of students were in their siestas, I went round to the school hall to see if it was ready for a school activity later that afternoon. Behind the curtains, by the grand piano, things appeared to be going on that left all three of us embarrassed. Paddy was a close friend from Umuoji in the East, how could I report him and risk his being expelled? I looked at his partner with utter disbelief because I was sure she had led Paddy into this. For the rest of my student days at King's College, I would avoid this girl. She would however continue this relation- ship a year later after we had left school, when I shared a room

with Paddy in Obalende. Paddy's lady-friend would turn up at
our flat without warning and I would be obliged to leave our flat
for Paddy and her. I would go for long walks around the racecourse to give them space and would come back to find they were
still at it.

The rest of 1955 went by like other years. The upper sixth
form of Chigbo, Maduka, Onuogu, Adeyinka and Obi (Pongo)
would be sitting their final examinations, the HSC that Octo-
ber/November 1955. There was a sort of electricity in the air
because we were interested in how these examinations would be
conducted. The next year would be our turn. It went very well
and as they had done in the School Certificate examinations two
years earlier, they had excellent marks in their HSC results that
were posted on the school notice board. That December, they left
and it was a bit sad. Those of us left behind in the dormitories
spent our Christmas in Lagos as we had done every year for the
last five years. In the new year, we would be in the upper sixth
form and would be the most senior students at King's College.

Leaving King's College

The last two years at King's College – the lower and upper sixth forms – were incredibly busy and exciting. It was as if all of a sudden one had discovered oneself. It was a heady mixture of youth, enthusiasm and ambition. We had the world at our feet, or at least Nigeria. We could become anything we wanted to be, and in the process make Nigeria a modern and tolerant state. We were now old enough to understand how privileged we were to be at King's College. There was a very powerful old-boys' association that manifested itself once a year at the annual inter-house sports competition. Their members were heads of government ministries, powerful lawyers and judges at the high court. We were now members of one of the few institutions in Nigeria that were above tribal or ethnic loyalties. Our daily life was filled with all types of activities and I was pleased to belong to many. I was a member of the League of Bribe Scorners. I joined the Nigeria Red Cross and obtained my first aid certificate. I was a member of the debating society and also a member of the Straw Club, an exclusive club of friends that went on picnics together. The Straw Club for instance had its annual picnic at Ikoyi Park with girls invited from Queen's College. It was all very innocent in the beautiful botanical gardens with little streams that drained into the Lagos lagoon. The highlight of the day was to grab a stolen kiss from any of the girls from Queen's College. Ikoyi Park was a little nature wonderland and has today been converted into a built up estate called Park View Estate. The nice swamps and canals have all gone. We also went to bar beach on foot and had our pictures taken against the roaring wind from the Atlantic ocean.

That has also disappeared in a frenzy of sand-fill, creating the eyesore of today's waterlogged Victoria Island. I was also a member of the drama society and a founder member of the writers' club, where we wrote essays on any topic that interested us and circulated them among members. I was also in The photographic club. A number of students joined the Army cadet club which did not interest me at all. One member I remember well was Rotimi, who ended up a lieutenant general in the Nigerian Army. In addition to all these clubs where I held office in one form or another, I was also a house prefect. To this must be added various sporting activities – football, athletics, tennis and reserve member of the cricket team. I had made many friends among the younger students, people who looked up to me. It was thus not very difficult to turn into the life of a dandy. A number of my friends and I in the lower sixth form and below us would dress up in our finest gear on Sunday to impress the girls who visited the premises on that day. I was now a regular Sunday host for the visit of Rachel, the lady in white. She had visited me every Sunday since our first meeting in October 1955. Rachel's visit was the highlight of my week and I loved it. Like all beautiful things, our beautiful platonic relationship could not last forever. In the new year, she would sail to the United Kingdom to study to be a nurse! I had half expected that Rachel was too good to spend the rest of her time teaching primary school kids in Lagos. As was the custom in those days, anybody that was worth anything went abroad for further studies in England. Rachel had a fiancé who was already in London studying to be an accountant. She had never mentioned him before because I think she did not want to hurt my feelings.

Besides, visiting a young boy at King's College did not in any way alter or impede her love and wish to marry her fiancé in England. Nevertheless, I took the news of her impending departure badly. On Christmas Eve in 1955, I attended the midnight mass at the Holy Cross cathedral and saw Rachel after mass. It was very pleasant to speak to her again. During that Christmas holiday I was senior enough to be able to go out with a few 'wide boys' to a few seedy nightclubs just off Broad Street. The clubs were mostly drinking places with a resident band that played beautiful high life music. Of course the girlfriends of the band boys and local prostitutes were also in attendance. These places came alive at about 9.00 p.m. in a sulphurous atmosphere of cigarette smoke and booze. There were no drugs in those days, or if there were, we did not know of them. My friends and I were relatively green and we drank orange squash. Our main interest was frankly to enjoy the music and look at the local tarts. I do not remember any of us having the courage to ask the girls to dance because they looked as if they 'had men' for breakfast. We would leave these establishments around 11.00 p.m., in time to get back, on foot, to the school premises before midnight. New Year's Eve saw my friends and I at the Anglican cathedral on the marina. At the stroke of midnight my friends and I turned towards the port to watch fireworks from the berthed ships on Apapa Wharf. After that we strolled along the marina where whispering pine trees breathed a refreshing breeze from the ocean. The whole of the marina was strung out with coloured Christmas lights from the Anglican cathedral, past the governor's residence to Onikan. There were usually hundreds of people all along the route and no dangers. The exercise was to find out who stayed out longest on New Year's Eve.

We would break our walk by the governor's residence and turn up by the race course, a huge expanse of greenery and trees, right opposite King's College. Today, the racecourse is covered in concrete and known as the Tafawa Balewa Square, used for military parades. Perhaps one day there will be a revolutionary governor of Lagos State who will reconvert this square to the old beloved racecourse and replant the trees and grass!

The school year of 1955 ended with the publication of results of the Cambridge Higher School Certificate examinations for that year. The school had so many A students that it was reputedly the best results ever at King's College. People like Chigbo, Maduka, Adeyinka, Obi and Onuogu did very well. This was a challenge for my year, which would be promoted to the upper sixth form, our last year at school. We had some good students in the science stream, especially Sowemimo, who is today a professor of medicine at the Lagos College of Medicine, and Ibeziako who is also a medical doctor. Chigbo, Maduka, Adeyinka and their mates left at the end of 1955 and I personally felt a big vacuum in their absence. They were my best friends and also my seniors.

The year 1956 would see our class promoted to the upper sixth form. I was determined to do well in the Higher School Certificate examinations because that was the only way I could achieve my ambition of going to university. I was certain at this stage that I was university material. My family wanted me to do medicine because they felt it was a profession that made people rich.

Unfortunately, my gut feeling after a few years helping in first aid in the Red Cross was that I empathised too much with patients so that I would be in danger of being too attached to them if I became a doctor. This was to haunt me for two years as I did Botany and Zoology for the Higher School Certificate (HSC) that year. I convinced myself that I should persevere in the sciences and could in the end become an agricultural engineer or biochemist. Besides in those days, the Nigerian federal government awarded an annual scholarship to the best students to go to university. These courses would enable Nigerians to take over from the British when they left. Most of the courses in the arts, medicine and straight sciences could be done at the Nigerian University College, Ibadan (UCI). UCI was affiliated to London University at that time and awarded London University degrees. Thus in addition to choosing a career, my love life was in turmoil. 1956 was going to be a tough year and I wanted to be sure I was up to it. Any lingering regards that I may have had for my classmate, Miss Idris, were now over. I wanted to maximise the rest of my time with Rachel before she went to the UK. She would sail on the Elder Dempster Lines ship, *The Aureole* in May and we were now in February, a bare three months to go. We wrote nearly every day to each other for those remaining three months. I was not to experience such intense feelings until many years later when I got married. Rachel continued to visit me on Sundays. On one Sunday before she left, she brought me a picture of herself that I was to keep to remind me of her. She also jolted me by telling me that some relations of her fiancé had informed him in the UK that she had been seen visiting a 'small boy' at King's College. I asked her what her response had been. She said she had replied honestly and correctly that she had been visiting a lonely boy who had no relations in Lagos.

It was, she had replied, an innocent relationship because she was five years older than I was. Three years later I would bump into her by luck at the British Council residence in Hans

Crescent in London where she worked part time during the holiday. We could not believe how fate had once again thrown us together. She would however tell me that her fiancé was also an Igbo man. Many years later, I would learn that the whole family had to leave Lagos during the Nigerian civil war and took refuge in what was then Biafra, the husband being Igbo. One can only imagine the suffering they went through. Before the Nigerian civil war of 1967, cross-ethnic marriages were many and thrived. Did not the mother of my dear friend, George Spiropoulous, of Aba, an Igbo woman, not marry Dr Solanke, a Yoruba, and chief medical officer at Aba General Hospital, when George's Greek father died?

The newly crowned Queen Elizabeth II of England and her husband Prince Phillip visited Nigeria in 1956. This was a major occasion at which King's College would play a key role. King's College had been selected to put on a gymnastics show, together with other schools, at the racecourse for the queen. The racecourse was on the other side of the road from King's College and it was almost like our show. Lagos was spruced up and hung with fairy lights everywhere. It was like Christmas. Our school came in for special treatment. The Tudor-like administrative building was all repainted and the whole school was decorated with lights. On the appointed day, all the schools were assembled at the racecourse before 10 a.m. to avoid the midday sun. It was like the gatherings we had in the playing fields in Aba before I was eleven to celebrate Empire Day on the 24th May every year. In those days, the Resident of Owerri Province would declare May 24th a public holiday. We would assemble at school on this public holiday where we would sing the British national anthem. After that, we would retire to a free bazaar of rice and meat stew prepared by the school on the school's playing field and offered to us by the government of King George VI. Queen Elizabeth II, the daughter of King George VI had become queen on the death of her father. She and her husband, Prince Phillip, were visiting Nigeria, their largest African colony. It would be her first visit to Africa since becoming queen. They arrived in Governor Macpherson's Rolls Royce at the racecourse and quickly transferred into an open army jeep, driven by Colonel Aguiyi-Ironsi, the highest-ranking Nigerian officer in the Nigerian Army in those days.

Aguiyi-Ironsi would subsequently become the first Nigeria head of the Army. After the coup d'état of 1966 by young army officers led by Captain Nzeogwu, Ironsi would take over as military head of state. He would be assassinated eight months later in a counter coup led by Northern Nigerian officers. It was said in those days that the Northern officers felt that the 1966 coup d'état in which prominent politicians from the North, like Sir Ahmadu Bello and Sir Abubakar Tafawa Balewa had been killed, was an 'Igbo-inspired' coup d'état. Nigeria has never recovered since those days!

The reception for the queen at the racecourse went without a hitch and when it was all over, we walked around the racecourse in our splendid white uniforms with blue and white college ties. Even the girls wore ties! That evening, we also had a banquet at King's College, courtesy of the queen. It was like the old Empire Day celebrations all over again. The rest of the day was free and we even had a chance to go into town to admire the lighting decorations put up to welcome Queen Elizabeth II. There had never been anything like that in Nigeria and this visit was welcomed by most Nigerians. We were given the next school day off to recover from our efforts. It was splendid. With my sentimental life about to be disrupted with the impending trip of Rachel to the UK, getting a good HSC now became an obsession and for good reasons too. A good HSC would offer me the only chance I would have to go to university. My family did not have the money to pay for university education for me and so I needed to get a scholarship. The only way to get a scholarship was to be one of the top students in my year in Nigeria. The federal and regional governments were giving scholarships to the brightest students to study at universities with a view to having a pool of trained people to take over from the British when independence came. Already in 1955, the British were preparing our next-door neighbour, the Gold Coast, later on to be known as Ghana, for independence. Their leader, Kwame Nkrumah, was well known. The British boasted of how well they had prepared the Gold Coast for independence because they had a good civil service staffed with university graduates. Nigeria was next in line for independence and would need lots of university graduates to take over from the British. King's College students were in the front line for this opportunity.

We needed to get good university degrees. If my preferred profession could not be studied in Nigeria I would be sent abroad to study at a foreign university. Many of us wanted to study abroad if possible, because of the often-exaggerated stories of how wonderful Europe was. These were stories from our rich friends whose parents had sent them abroad to complete their sixth forms. Besides, my bosom friend, Benji Maduka, had already in early 1955 decamped to Germany and was now registered at the University of Heidelberg where he was studying Philosophy.

I settled down to a scholastic regime of Physics, Chemistry, Botany and Zoology. Each subject had a serious laboratory side that exceeded anything we had done before. In Zoology for example, we no longer dissected insects like cockroaches. Now we had to dissect frogs and mice! In Physics, we did experiments on surface tension. Our teachers were very much on top of their jobs and drilled us for the forthcoming examinations.

On the sports field, the school was more ambitious. A combined team of footballers, cricketers and tennis players was sent to compete with Government College Ibadan and later in the year went to Achimota College in the Gold Coast to compete with them. To qualify for the school team, you had to play reasonably well in all three games. Cricket stars like Sonny Akpata were automatically in the team if he could not play tennis or football. By contrast, people like Nkune who played all three sports well, were the natural leaders of the group. I got into the team because I was good in football and fairly good in tennis. I had learnt to play tennis at King's College.

I was the reserve in cricket, should any member of the team fall ill. At Government College Ibadan, we were fed with black-eyed beans just hours before our football match. As every Nigerian knows, black-eyed beans literally sit heavily in the stomach and sends one to sleep. Our football team was sluggish on the pitch and I think we lost. We thrashed them though in tennis and cricket. So much for gamesmanship.

The school team's trip to the Gold Coast was extraordinary. For a start it was the first trip out of Nigeria for most of us. We went in a truck (not a bus) along the main coastal road, next to the Atlantic ocean, passing Dahomey (now Benin) and Togo on the way. It took a whole day to make the trip. Today it takes no more than four hours to do the same journey. We arrived at Achimota College exhausted. What we saw though was a college that rivalled King's College in every way. Achimota students were self-assured, cleanly turned out and very polite. The premises were in a purpose built campus that was larger than King's College and very clean. I cannot remember how well we did but I remember us being terrified by their reputation and feeling slightly inferior.

In May 1956 Rachel sailed to the UK. We were in class and in mid-morning at about 11 a.m. we heard the siren of *The Aureole* as it signalled its departure. We knew the sirens of the different ships because so many of our friends from wealthy families sailed to the UK every month to continue their studies. Poor us would listen for the siren on that date and would look at each other in class as the sound pierced through.

I wonder what our teachers made of the glancing around. And so as the ship carrying Rachel sounded its siren, everybody in my class turned around to look at me with a sort of sheepish smile of, 'there goes the sweetheart of loverboy'. I have to admit I was sad but smiled all the same in order not to be thought of as 'wet'. At least that crisis was over and I could now concentrate on my HSC. July 1956 came and we were off for the long vacation, the last for me at King's College. We made the usual four-days'-journey to the East. A few other senior students and myself looked after the junior students. Two Aba boys, Ibegbulam and Strongface, a year below me, were on the train also. These two would be the only other boys from Aba to enter King's College in over ten years, after Benji Maduka and myself had done so in 1950.

Our arrival in Aba provoked the same enthusiasm and joy in seeing one's parents and relations as had been the case on my first vacation in 1950. This time however, I would spend those three months in Aba going through all my notes in readiness for the HSC examination that would take place in November. I worked hard and saw my friends when I needed a break. My friends would visit me in my special room in our house in Aba. We would drink lots of orange squash and would head for the guesthouse near the railway station, in the European quarter of town. We were now sophisticated and I had been in smarter department stores and clubs in Lagos than they had in Aba. We were healthy adolescents of eighteen to nineteen years old and dressed to kill! Some evenings we got together and put on the suits that we had had made locally and went to the local photographic studios where we had our pictures taken. I still have those pictures today.

The big line in style in 1956 was that your trousers had to have a 'double fish' of very deep pleats in front, so that the trousers looked like a girl's skirt, but tight in the middle. The trouser material had to be a mixture of wool and nylon so that it moved in the wind. It had to be a light blue or grey in colour. We were *à la mode* and we dressed to show it.

After the long vacation of 1956, I returned to King's College in September and to serious work in readiness for the HSC examinations. Every other interest – girlfriends, sports – was pushed aside to study for these examinations. With Rachel away to the United Kingdom, I took no further interest in girls at college. Our teachers were also excellent. We did a mock examination with old HSC papers in every subject. The great day arrived in early November and as we sat on individual desks in the school's great assembly hall, we knew the day of our destinies had arrived. The papers arrived in sealed envelopes. The examination supervisors were our actual subject teachers and opening the large brown envelopes was the first time they had set eyes on the papers. When all the papers had been put down on the desk, face downwards, the order to turn our papers over was given by the teacher sitting on the high desk in front of us. He also announced the duration of the paper, usually one hour or, more likely, 90 minutes. There were usually two or three other teachers assisting the main examiner. We never heard of anyone cheating or of examination papers being leaked in advance, a common occurrence in other less privileged institutions. I was nervous but not excessively so. When time was up, the examiner would shout stop, after of course letting us know in advance when we had just five minutes to the end.

I made certain I left immediately after every paper because I could not stand the students who wanted to discuss how well they had handled certain questions. I went straight back to the dormitory to get ready for the next paper. All the theoretical papers were done in the first week and the practical examinations the week after.

And so for the next ten days, the science upper sixth class did our examinations for the Higher School Certificate. My examinations were in Physics, Chemistry, Botany, Zoology and Advanced English. Paradoxically, my most difficult paper was Advanced English. By the end of the second week of the examinations, we were pretty exhausted. After all, we were putting in the performance of a lifetime. Those results would determine our future. On the third week, the practical examinations in the sciences – Physics, Chemistry, Botany and Zoology were to take place. By now, most or us knew reasonably well how we had fared in the examinations.

I was reasonably confident that I had passed, and the only question was the grades that I would get. I went into the final week for the practical examinations with a bounce in my feet. That helped because I sailed through the practical examinations. It was all over, and in a matter of weeks I would leave King's College forever. The end came very quickly, in December 1956.

We had an excellent Christmas lunch at which we bade farewells to colleagues and friends from the junior classes. It was a strange parting experience. There were no great tears because we all felt we were going to see each other again as part of this great family of present students and the King's College old-boys' association, the KCOB. One other reason for not being sentimental about parting was that almost all my classmates who had just finished the HSC examinations had also filled forms in the second term of 1956 applying for scholarships for university education. We also had written to various universities in Nigeria and abroad, seeking to know the conditions for admission to courses in the new year. We now had to wait until the new year to see if we were successful in our scholarship applications.

In addition to that, most of us, and especially those students from the East, had applied for jobs in the Lagos area to start in the new year of 1957. These would be our first paid employment. If you were from the East, you had to stay on in Lagos because that was where all the decisions were made and also the centre of government. Rushing home to be with family was not an option. We were thus very busy and did not have much time to be tearful or to reflect that we would soon be leaving an institution that had shaped our lives. On the last day of school, my classmates and I returned to school to bid farewell to our teachers and housemasters. These people had made us what we were and we knew it! That Christmas and new year were the last I would celebrate in King's College. Early in the new year I moved out of the school's boarding house and lodged temporarily with some friend from the year before me.

I spent probably two weeks or so with this friend whose name I cannot now remember, while I looked for my own apartment. I concentrated my search in the Obalende part of Lagos. At the same time, I had to go back to King's College to see if I had a letter offering me appointment, albeit for a temporary period before going up to university.

In mid-January 1957, I received a letter offering me employment as junior staff at the Nigerian radio network called the Nigerian Broadcasting Service, NBS. My job would entail being behind consoles to assist a broadcaster in cueing in music from discs or recorded programmes from magnetic tapes. We worked in shifts of eight hours each – morning, afternoon and the late evening shift of 3.00 p.m. to 11.00 p.m. when the station shut down. I was also successful in finding a single room lodging in Obalende. The price was too high for an individual, so I had to find a flatmate willing to share with me. I invited my old school mate, Patrick (Paddy) Ekpunobi to share the one-room apartment with me. Paddy had also just been offered a job for the Nigeria Broadcasting Service. Paddy joined me in our new residence and brought in his own bed. We each had a bed that we placed against the opposite walls of our room. A gas stove mounted on a table in one corner of the room was the kitchen. We hung our clothes on metal hangers that we swung on a rope strung across the room. We used curtains to hide our beds and clothes from the central area that served as the living area. This was where we received visitors. In order to avoid any conflicts, we did not share anything. Each of us had his own pot, cooked his meals separately, bought his own soap separately, etc. This way, we did not have any quarrel or argument whatsoever, except for the notorious visit by Paddy's old King's College girlfriend. When she came, I walked the streets of Obalende and the racecourse until she left. Sometimes, I had to be out for two to three hours and that was not nice at all.

My seniors like Adeyinka, Chigbo, Obi, Onuogu and Maduka had gone on to university. Chigbo, Obi and Onuogu went to University College Ibadan, while Maduka had gone on to Leeds University in the United Kingdom. I visited my friends in Ibadan to see how they lived and saw the very comfortable halls of residence. Every student had his own room, a considerable upgrade in comfort after the dormitories of King's College. I was glad to see them again. Back to Lagos, we continued our routine of work shifts at the NBS. I was meanwhile recruited into their cricket team that was well known in Lagos for the social standing of its members. The captain was no less than Major J C Allen, a retired major of the British Army and personnel director of the Nigerian Broadcasting Service. He was a tall broad-shouldered man with an officer's moustache. A dashing man, he wore bow ties or cravats with his impeccably ironed white long-sleeved shirts. Major Allen was famous for the piano concerts he gave in his magnificent mansion in Ikoyi and was a great patron of music in Lagos. Once there was a piano recital by some famous pianist from London at the central Lugard Hall in Lagos, and he invited me and other youngsters to attend. This was my first ever visit to a concert hall. We met in his house before the concert began and were ferried to the concert in his Rolls Royce. That was also the first Rolls Royce ride of my life.

In addition to riding in his Rolls Royce, Major Allen had decided that I could play the piano and that he would teach me on the grand piano in his living room. After all, one or two child piano prodigies were regular visitors to his place where he coached them. After the fourth or fifth lesson, I 'chickened' out when I realised quite simply I did not have the talent. I continued to play cricket with the NBS cricket club in which Major Allen was the wicket-keeper. These were truly wonderful days. I was twenty plus, awaiting my HSC results, a bit of money in my post office account and believing firmly that the future of Nigeria depended on us, the young.

At Broadcasting House we met stars of Nigerian drama, religion and literature. Chinua Achebe, later to become one of Nigeria's most famous writers, was head of the drama department at NBS when I worked there as an interim in 1957. This was a relatively happy time. For one, I actually earned money (£12 per month) and was able to buy new clothes for myself and have decent pocket money. I could not go on wearing my school uniform to work. For one thing, those beautiful girls of King's College fame, Etuk and Udoaffia, were now at the NBS. In addition, there were also some very intelligent and attractive girls from other colleges, working as interim students at the same time as us at NBS. If you were on an early morning shift, you made the lonely trip at 5.00 a.m., past the Ikoyi cemetery, in order to open transmission at 6.00 a.m. with Christian or Moslem prayers.

Occasionally, your companion on this wretched shift would be a girl. With time, you got to know each other, especially if you had to go home at the same time when your morning shift ended at 12.00 for the day. And that way I met a very sweet girl from the old mid-west region of Nigeria, who I shall call Cecilia. The relationship lasted the good part of a year and would prove to be rather painful. Cecilia was in love and wrote to me some of the most beautiful love letters I would ever receive in my life. I was very fond of her but I was not in love with her. It was rather a pity and had all to do with the timing – my preoccupations at this time were frankly getting a good HSC result and a government scholarship to go to university. Everything else, including my job at Broadcasting House, was temporary and of limited significance. I tried to limit the damage we would do to each other because I was convinced it would not work. Many years later, I was lucky to see her again as a married woman and mother of several children. She had done very well with her life and was very successful!

In late January 1957, the HSC results arrived from the United Kingdom and were posted on the school's main board. Word got round that they had arrived and I rushed round from my job at the NBS to see. The results exceeded my expectations. I had A's in my four principal subjects – Physics, Chemistry, Botany and Zoology. The best HSC result in Nigeria that year was by Sowemimo, my classmate. I came second in the whole of Nigeria but top in Zoology, and won the prize for the best Zoology student – a dissecting set. These results gave me confidence in my abilities. There were however, two more hurdles to jump – a scholarship and admission to the university of my choice.

The first of these dilemmas was to be resolved around June 1957, six months after I had started working. The Nigeria *Daily Times* newspaper, the major daily of the country, carried a report in which the regional scholarship boards of the North, the Eastern and Western Nigeria had published the winners of regional government scholarships for 1957. I had been offered a scholarship to study Agricultural Chemistry for three years at University College, Ibadan. Courses were to start in October 1957. I was pleased that at least I had a course I could do if the worst came to the worst, but it was not my first choice. I was more suited to Medicine, the career that my father wanted. They said you become rich as a doctor, because you earn a lot of money. But I did not fancy the length of time it took to complete – six years. Besides, my time in the Nigerian Red Cross had put me off the sight of blood and suffering, after I saw a child break his arm after falling off a tree in a playground. In my application for a federal government scholarship, my subject of choice was simply Industrial Chemistry. The idea that I would learn how to run complex chemical processes, the very heart of modern life, appealed to me. Not many people in Nigeria did a course like that and no university in Nigeria offered it. I was quite nervous at this time because I did not have much time left to accept or reject the offer of an Agricultural Chemistry scholarship from the eastern regional government, the region of my birth. On the other hand, I was awaiting the result of my application for a federal government scholarship before I could decide what course to follow. The federal government scholarship awards would come out around September 1957 and I would be relieved to see my name in the list of successful applicants.

This singular event would completely change my life again as my entrance to King's College had, seven years earlier. My scholarship was awarded to study Industrial Chemistry at the Institute of Science and Technology of the University of Manchester. Today, this institute is known as the University of Manchester Institute of Science and Technology (UMIST) and is one of the top four technology universities of the UK. The second of my three tasks had now been solved. What remained was whether UMIST would admit me based on my HSC results.

I had to worry because I had not offered mathematics in my HSC. The offer of a place at Manchester would arrive in October 1957 for a place in the Honours BSc. Chemistry class beginning in October 1958. That was nice but also galling. I would spend the next twelve months in Lagos, fiddling at the NBS instead of studying Chemistry. Besides, I was now twenty-one and would arrive in Manchester at the grand old age of twenty-two instead of nineteen or twenty years old. I was of course pleased that I had more or less achieved my ambition up till this stage. I would be able to meet again some of my best friends, Benjamin Maduka, Adebayo Ajao, Vincent Maduka, etc, who had all gone away to study abroad. Some luckier ones had gone all the way to the United States, although there were some eyebrows raised when people returned to Nigeria with American degrees. Nigerian undergraduates were to be found in universities at the four corners of the world. There were students in the old Soviet Union, Canada, New Zealand and Australia. It was as if the Nigerian government of the day had been inspired by the same vision as the Meiji emperors of Japan in the nineteenth century, to send their best students to the West to acquire Western science and technology and to return and transform Japan.

We were filled with a singular mission in those days – to obtain the Golden Fleece and then return to transform Nigeria. Ghana after all became independent that year, with Kwame Nkrumah as its first prime minister. We were filled with pride, and the greatest joy in those halcyon days in 1957 was to listen to Radio Ghana from 6.30 a.m. to 7.00 a.m. every morning. It broadcast a non-stop diet of high-life music played by E T Mensah, the father of high life music. All the little portable radios

in Obalende were on the same frequency and what you heard was
whole streets of the same music. If you were taking your bath
from a bucket of water or preparing your breakfast of maize pap
and bean balls or fried plantains, you simply had to make room to
listen to these incredibly beautiful dance rhythms that were a
mixture of Cuban beats and African rhythms. After that, going to
work at the NBS was a pleasure. We had no equivalent to E T
Mensah at NBS in those days.

By the end of 1957, I had achieved most of what I had hoped
for at this stage in my life. I now had a place at Manchester
University and almost a year to get ready. The next stage in my
life would also prove dramatic and worrying. After all, the true
stories of what life was really like for Nigerian students abroad
were finally trickling back to Nigeria. A good number were
destitute, without money to complete their studies. Some had lost
it and literally gone mad and had to be repatriated to Nigeria.
There was real anxiety but I wanted to find out for myself.

I did not believe that London was all paved with gold, but I
was determined to push myself to the utmost limit of my
intellectual capabilities and I felt the only place I could do it then
was at a university in the United Kingdom. For my parents, the
anxieties and sadness of 1950 when I left Aba for King's College,
Lagos would be repeated all over again. This time, it would be
even worse because I would be away, abroad in Europe, with no
hope of them seeing me for a minimum of three years, maybe six.
Would I be changed irremediably and no longer accept them and
their way of life? These were fair questions because my father
already had some experience of sending young people abroad to
study. In 1948, my father was the secretary general of Akokwa
Town Union and was responsible for collecting money from our
townspeople to pay for the sponsorship of two people from
Akokwa to study in the United States.

The two people were Elechukwu Njaka and William (Willie)
Okefie-Uzoaga. They both distinguished themselves obtaining
doctorate degrees in politics and finance. Elechukwu ended up as
a member of the old Eastern House of Assembly. Willie rose to
the post of professor and head of department of Finance at the
University of Nigeria in Nsukka. Willie's signature was the

guarantor on the back of the notes of Biafra during the Nigerian civil war. I had seen these two gentlemen in our house in Aba when they came to collect their money and sign pledges of how to help Akokwa after their studies. They did help Akokwa when they returned, but not in the way the village people expected. I think they were expected to make the government bring roads, water and factories to Akokwa.

Of course they were not able to do that. Dr K O Mbadiwe, representing Arondizuogu that shared a boarder with Akokwa, was already in place as a federal minister in Lagos. So what could the two poor fellows from Akokwa accomplish? All this was to weigh heavily on my parents as they celebrated the good fortune of not having to pay for my university education. My departure for the United Kingdom and Manchester University would not be until late August 1958. Until then I had to resign from my job at the Nigerian Broadcasting Service and say goodbye to my new work friends in Lagos.

I had saved quite a bit of money from the fifteen months I had worked in Lagos. This would give me the chance to buy some smart clothes from the Union Trading Company, UTC shop on the marina in Lagos. UTC was Swiss and had Italian-made clothes that cost more and looked better than those at Kingsway Stores which was essentially British. I needed at least one good suit for going to the UK and I saved most of my earnings for a good part of fifteen months to purchase it at UTC. It was a lovely dark grey suit. I also bought a sparkling white shirt with a burgundy red tie to match. I remember the details because I went to a photographic studio soon after I bought them and had a photograph taken. It was a wonderful period for me because I knew I was now on a new route to a new experience in my life. It would be as dramatic as the day in 1950 when I set off from Aba in Eastern Nigeria to go to King's College. It would be even lonelier as I would be nearly 6,000 kilometres away and in a different climatic zone.

I would be living among the British, the ruling colonial power in Nigeria in 1958. Would they be as nice as the English teachers we had met at King's College in Lagos? My immediate priorities were to pack my things and return to Aba, in the East, to bid farewell to my family.

I left Lagos by train in mid-July and returned to Aba, travelling over the familiar route from West to East via Northern Nigeria. It took the usual three nights and four days but I have no memory of this trip. I was understandably absorbed with going abroad to study Industrial Chemistry at Manchester University. When I arrived in Aba my parents collected me as usual from the railway station. The next day I saw a half-page advert in the local daily that Gabriel Ibekwe, my father, would be giving a farewell party for his son Samuel Ibekwe at the Akokwa Union Hall in Cameron Road, Aba. The party was to celebrate the departure of his son to the United Kingdom for further studies. This was not my style as I was always a shy young man. And so I protested. Our family friends promptly told me that the party was not necessarily for me, although I would be there. It was more of a statement for my father and the Akokwa Union in Aba. My father had for eleven years been the secretary general of the Akokwa Union in our village. As such, he wanted the other Igbo communities in Aba to know that they, the Akokwa people, also had a son going abroad to study. I really did not figure very much in the equation and it could be anybody else from Akokwa going abroad. My father, his friends and family put on a very good party in a huge community hall. There was quite a lot of rice and meat stew to eat. A local catering company did the cooking.

Gallons of locally brewed palm wine and beer were drunk. Towards the end of the meeting, the chairman for the occasion made a speech telling everyone why we were there. Several dignitaries stood up to congratulate my father on what he had done for me and for our community. My father made a following speech thanking everyone for coming to the party. At the end of it all, it was my turn to make a speech, and it had to be in Igbo. I was no longer fluent in Igbo after seven years of being at King's College in Lagos. It was an ordeal and although I did not panic, I found it difficult. There was an audience of over 500 people in a hot sticky hall in Aba. They were principally interested in hearing me say that I would come back to their community after my studies abroad, to help them. Coming back home after studying abroad and respecting them and their customs was very important to them. They deeply resented young Igbo people who had studied abroad and, when they returned home, turned their backs on them and their customs. Of course I promised all this because I did not really know what I would find abroad at this stage.

Besides, it did not make any sense to disappoint all these people who in a strange manner were sublimating their desires for their own children through me. There was so much optimism – not jealousy – on their faces, that one of theirs had made it. Alfred who had worked for my father, and who sixteen years ago had carried me, a screaming brat, to start school at Christ the King School, Aba, was there. He told me how proud he was of me! I had made promises to these people, albeit people who were not in my family, but I felt a sense of obligation to them. This would make a significant impact on my adolescent life many years later.

My going-away party at the Akokwa Union Hall, Aba, was carried in the local daily newspaper. From then on, Aba people knew that I was on my way to the United Kingdom to study Industrial Chemistry. I could not now drop out or come back to Nigeria without a university degree. That was some pressure! But then, as my father would later tell me, 'You must cope with any pressures you feel because people before you have gone down that path. You will not be the first to do so.' That just about sealed my fate. I would spend the next few weeks saying goodbye to uncles and aunts in our village of Akokwa and to my friends and their parents in Aba. I had already done most of my purchase of tropical clothing in Lagos. We had been told by the secretariat in Lagos that our scholarship included an allowance (money) for purchasing winter clothing when we arrived in the UK. The only thing left was a Nigerian national dress. My father had a flowing dress in white lace made in the Yoruba Agbada style. I tried it on and it looked magnificent. Subsequently I wore it no more than three times in my six years in the United Kingdom. I did not feel comfortable in it, probably because I did not feel any special need to show my nationalism.

In Search of the Golden Fleece

In early September 1958, the family and other close relations assembled at our house in 86 Clifford Road, Aba, to accompany me to Port Harcourt, a distance of about 60 kilometres from Aba. Our local airport was at Port Harcourt and from there I would fly to Lagos for the journey to the United Kingdom. Finished was the four-day trip by train to Lagos. Time was now precious.

I wore a suit with tie and had one suitcase of clothes and books. The suitcase was made entirely of leather and had been imported from Portugal. My father had purchased it from the market in Aba and today, forty years later, my most precious objects are kept in this very same leather suitcase. The visit to Port Harcourt airport was my first visit ever to the inside of an airport. I had seen the airport in Ikeja, Lagos, but had never been inside. I arrived with my family and their friends at the airport in a sort of motorcade of about six cars, mostly rented. My father had briefly owned a second-hand Austin car that broke down so often that he had to get rid of it. At the small airport building, I bought my ticket to Lagos and then came back to sit with my family and their friends. It was all very solemn because my parents and their friends had turned out in their best clothing. I listened to the last bits of advice from everyone else except my parents.

My father was clearly proud of his son and in consequence said little or nothing. My mother was near to tears at the thought of me going abroad for three years or maybe even more. When I was at King's College, Lagos, she saw me once a year for three months. Now she would not see me for years. The departure of our flight to Lagos was announced and I immediately checked my boarding pass, my other tickets for the flight from Lagos to London and my little carry-on business bag. I hugged everybody and kissed my mother goodbye amid her tears. Our aeroplane was a small Dakota DC3 propeller plane owned by Nigerian Airways. The pilot in those days was almost always a European. We were no more than about fifteen passengers to board the flight, mostly expatriate Europeans working on the newly discovered crude petrol in the Port Harcourt delta. I sat by a window from which I could see my parents. Soon the doors of the aircraft were shut and the air hostess, a very smartly dressed Nigerian girl, handed us some fruity sweets. I asked what they were about and I was told that when the aircraft pulled up, our eardrums would suffer, and sucking sweets would lessen the pain. Just as I was taking in this new information, our dear hostess reappeared, this time with little balls of cotton wool. We were to stuff these into our ear holes throughout the flight because our Dakota was very noisy and could damage our hearing! Soon the plane pulled off to the runway and began to taxi to the take-off point. It ran down the runway and pulled up, as noisily as the air hostess had predicted. I looked down and saw my parents and their friends disappear as tiny dots in the horizon. My new life was about to begin. The flight to Lagos, a distance of 450 kilometres, took about two hours in our Dakota.

We flew low thus giving me my first aerial view of the Niger delta from Port Harcourt in the East to Ikeja in the West. It was a marvellous sight – the rivers, the forests, and the little fishing villages all along the edge of the Atlantic ocean. This flight showed me how immense Nigeria was and how thinly populated the hinterland was. We landed in early evening in Lagos at about 6 p.m. and I waited to collect my one and only suitcase. From the domestic terminal I moved on to the international terminal, all within the same building. When I look back now, I must say I was pretty sure of what I was doing because I do not remember having to ask anybody where I should report. The airport was of course small in those days and the number of overseas flights limited. I do remember that we had to connect that same night with a British Overseas Airways Corporation (BOAC) plane for London. We checked in at the counter for London and were given our boarding passes. Two hours later we boarded our plane, a huge plane, and at least the largest I had ever seen until then. It was a strato-cruiser, a sort of turbo-jet, the precursors to today's jet aircraft. We took off at around midnight into the dark Lagos sky. Soon the plane was over the Atlantic Ocean over Lagos harbour where it turned round to head north for the Sahara desert and Europe. We must have been over 120 passengers.

Two hours into our flight, the pilot announced over the loudspeaker that we had hit a sandstorm at the edge of the Sahara desert. The plane tossed everyone up and down. Sitting next to me was an Anglican priest who went into full-time prayer for deliverance from disaster. Our plane was forced to turn back due to the severity of the storm. The pilot could not see very far.

We turned back but could not land at Lagos airport. The airport was already shut for the night. The pilot informed us that he was diverting to Accra airport in the newly independent Ghana. We spent some time in Ghana and then took off again. This time, we had a pleasant flight and stopped over in an attractively lit-up city in North Africa. Today, I know that the nicely lit-up city we landed in was Tripoli in Libya, then ruled by King Idris. We had landed in the early hours of the morning and it was freezing. We were ushered into a restaurant at the airport where Arab waiters in red tunic jackets and black trousers served us. They looked very smart. The only Arabs I had seen before these were Lebanese and Syrian traders in Nigeria.

We had a breakfast of fried eggs with toast and tea. Soon after, we boarded our flight again for London and landed early evening at Heathrow airport to a cold, wet and dark London in late September. As we came through the immigration, a gracious English lady called out the names of those of us who would spend a week with the British Council in London. We were foreigners but we were special! We were collected with our baggage and directed to a bus. About twenty of us mounted the bus and headed for West London in the mist and fog for our first night at the British Council residence in Lancaster Gate. There we would spend another week to learn how to adjust to life in England! It was all like going to King's College, Lagos from Aba, but with a difference. The weather was unkind and cold and that took getting used to. The locals were not exactly cheering, but there was no hostility. This combined coolness of both the weather and people was very strange because coming from King's College, which was more or less like an English boarding school, I expected people to react like we had known at King's College.

In addition to that I saw my first Englishman cleaning the street and another asking for money. These were confusing signals because none of these incidents fitted the image I had of Britain before I left Nigeria. Later that week, after a series of orientation courses at the British Council, we would make our first excursion to the underground rail network, the tube. This was not so easy to comprehend for anyone used to overland trains that ran at no more than thirty-five kilometres per hour.

We would be taken also to Marks and Spencer (M&S) in Baker Street in London to buy our winter clothes. I bought a pair of long johns for the cold winter days and they were to serve me well for many years. I always wondered what the sales staff at M&S made of us – ten or so, buying woollen clothes all at the same time. By the end of that first week I felt rather lonely and decided to seek out a friendly and familiar face that would help me settle down. I sought out my childhood friend, Benjamin Maduka, who, as I said earlier, had by then been in London for nearly a year. Benji came to the British Council residence in Lancaster Gate to collect me. I was so glad to see him again. We had both achieved our dreams of getting a university education, and doing so abroad. Something in Benji's behaviour, however, worried me. He was no longer the carefree young man I knew in Nigeria. He was much more serious and smiled less. Later on, I would visit Benji's lodgings in Swiss Cottage where a kindly old Jewish woman that had escaped the Nazis in Germany and was starting a new life in England, looked after him. The terraced house on four floors was a bit old but perfectly habitable. Benji introduced me to his landlady, who made tea for us.

It was the landlady who told me that Benji was thinking of moving over to Heidelberg University in Germany where he had been given a place to study Philosophy. Benji's landlady could not understand how anybody would want to leave London to study in Germany where she had suffered so much. This meeting made me realise that Benji was probably having problems with money. He was not on a scholarship and he had to wait every month for money to be sent to London by his father from Aba. What a way to live! No wonder he no longer looked carefree.

During this short stay in London, I also ran into Rachel by

sheer chance, as she was working at the British Council in their library as a part-time holiday student. I was so glad to see her again. She also seemed happy to see me but was a bit reserved. Was this what going to the UK did to people? We went into the canteen and she offered me tea with cakes. We talked and laughed and I was happy again. Gradually, she let me know that she was now married to her fiancé and that they had settled down. She had had a difficult time explaining to her fiancé who the little boy at King's College, Lagos was and that there had been nothing serious between herself and me. That was true, but it hurt. She then said 'You have always said you loved me and would do anything for my happiness. Well, if you care about me, I kindly ask you to give me back all the letters I wrote to you and my photo, in order to protect my marriage.' I was stunned and for a few minutes did not know what to say. My eyes filled with tears as she looked at me. I turned to her and said, 'Yes, I will give them back to you.' I went to my room and collected all her letters and the one and only picture I had of her. I came down and handed them over to her.

She thanked me and gave me a firm and prolonged hug – not a kiss. That day she left my life forever and I never saw her again. Two weeks later, I boarded a train at Euston Station in London for the long journey north to Manchester where I would start a new life as a foreign student. My Igbo childhood would be effectively over. I would join English and other foreign students to life in a hall of residence in Manchester and a university course in honours Chemistry in immense lecture halls where 120 students would sit in to lectures at 9 a.m. on the nature of chemical bonds between atoms!

The Return to Nigeria

In 1965, I left the United Kingdom on an Elder Dempster Line ship from Liverpool for Nigeria, immediately after my studies, in order to serve my country that had provided me with a scholarship. I had obtained a doctorate degree in Chemistry from the University of Manchester and I was full of idealism on how to help lift my country from poverty. Our ship left Liverpool in the dark mist of a February morning in 1965. For three days, the journey was pleasant, with good food and entertainment. Most of the passengers were expatriate British officers returning from leave in the United Kingdom and a sprinkling of West African students returning to their countries after their studies abroad. On the fourth day, we hit the Azores, off the coast of Portugal. The ship's decks were empty except for staff. Most of the passengers were seasick! Apparently, the sea is always rough in the Azores and nobody had warned us. It took another forty-eight hours for most people to recover and venture out on deck. From then on it was like a pleasure boat. Close relationships were formed and broken, as one would expect with people cooped up together for close on two weeks.

Our first port of call after the Azores was Las Palmas in the Canary Islands, off the coast of Morocco. Las Palmas then had a reputation in West Africa as a prostitute's paradise and many a man had lost his wallet in the narrow streets of the town. We were let out for half a day there. I went into town with two Nigerians returning from their studies in the UK. I have to admit that I was neither impressed nor tempted. I was more interested in the reception awaiting me at home after six years' absence. Our ship later stopped in Freetown – Sierra Leone, Monrovia – Liberia and Accra – Ghana. By now it was getting steadily hotter. Besides, I was not prepared for the tin roofs of the houses in the ports of these West African cities. It was my first experience of what is now known as 'culture shock'. In the end, I shrugged it off. After all I was returning to the newly independent Nigeria for which I had trained so hard in the United Kingdom.

I had two job offers in hand – one was as a lecturer in Inorganic Chemistry at the University of Nigeria, Nsukka, Enugu, the east regional capital of Nigeria. The other was as a research chemist at the Federal Institute of Industrial Research FIIRO, Oshodi, Lagos. I chose the Lagos job in order to be near the centre of activities. During my absence in the United Kingdom, Nigeria had gained its independence from Britain on October 1, 1960 and had become a federal republic on October 1, 1963. Everybody had tremendous hopes for Nigeria. There were so many trained Africans and besides, oil in commercial quantities was beginning to flow from Nigeria's wells.

Our ship docked in Apapa, Lagos after thirteen days' voyage. A cousin was at the quayside to welcome me. Later that day, I caught an internal flight to Port Harcourt to meet my parents and a retinue of well-wishers who had come from Aba (60 kilometres away) to welcome me. My proud father and mother were there to welcome me, six years after I last saw them. There were a few tears of joy after which we left in a motorcade for Aba to a huge reception that my father had organised. People from my village of Akokwa and Aba friends of my father gathered in a town hall and speeches were made to which I was asked to respond.

I had lost my fluency in the Igbo language even more after six years in the United Kingdom. More worrying was the look of expectation on the faces of the people who had turned up. I was going to lead them out of ignorance and poverty and I knew I did not have the power to achieve that! Later, we retired to our 86 Clifford Road residence that had by then been converted into a modern concrete building with corrugated sheet for roofing. My father gave me a room with an adjoining living room. For four days, a string of visitors, male and female, young and old, trouped to our place to see the young man who had returned from the United Kingdom with a doctorate degree. It was not that common in those days. My mother took great pride in announcing to me who the next visitor was and why I must be very polite to them. A week later, my family and I left Aba for our village, Akokwa, to repeat the welcome process. This time, I had to go to mass at the local Saint Barnabas Catholic church where my father and mother offered a thanksgiving mass. My parents were very proud and so were my Auntie Maggie and my uncle, Chief Mathias Okafor.

Through all this I had the odd feeling that I was expected to show tangible physical evidence in the future of my new-found status, by throwing money around to all and sundry. Little did they know that I would start work as a civil servant with no possibilities to enrich myself!

In April 1965, I went back to Lagos and started work as a research chemist at the Federal Institute of Industrial Research in Lagos. My job was to find local substitutes to imported indigo dye. Indigo dying was known in Northern Nigeria for hundreds of years and was obtained from a locally grown plant. My job was to find a method of extracting this dyestuff from lorry-loads of leaves that used to be delivered to the centre. Technically, there was no real problem in the concept, but how do you use hundreds of litres of highly volatile solvents like diethyl ether in a laboratory with a room temperature of about 35°C? We persevered but the quantities extracted were insufficient to make the process commercial. It was cheaper to import Chinese manufactured indigo. I was allocated a residence that went with the post, a beautiful bungalow in the government residential area in Ikeja. Nigerian and European professionals lived side by side and it was rather nice.

My colleagues at work were no other than my seniors from King's College – Gilbert Chigbo and Segun Adeyinka. They helped me settle into the new Nigeria. I also caught up with my kindergarten soulmate, Georgie Spiropoulous, who was by now a mechanical engineer working in Lagos for a multinational company. It was a good time to be in Lagos. There was little or no violence and no power cuts.

We had fabulous parties at the weekend and American Peace Corps personnel were invited. Below the surface however, there appeared to be some unease creeping into our newly gained independence. The talk at parties was of corruption of ministers and the paralysis of government. At the federal level, Dr Nnamdi Azikiwe from the East was made the first Nigerian governor general and subsequently the first president. Sir Abubakar Tafawa Balewa from the North was the federal prime minister and had real power. In the North, Sir Ahmadu Bello was the prime minister and was seen by many as the real power broker in Nigeria. In the West, Chief Obafemi Awolowo was the prime minister and in the East, Dr Michael Okpara took over the premiership of the East when Dr Azikiwe went to Lagos to become the president. There was a palpable malaise that things were not going too well between the four power centres of the three regions and the central government.

On January 15, 1966, a group of army officers overthrew the government at about 2 a.m. I had given a party the night before in my Ikeja residence. Everything came to a standstill. That afternoon, by pure chance, I had already been booked to fly out from Lagos on a French airline, UTA, for Paris. I had been offered a Research fellowship in Chemistry to work under a famous chemist of the time, Professor Joe Chatt, at the University of Sussex in England. My salary would be £1,200 per year. I took the chance and got out because there was the fear that we were heading for a civil war and that the Igbos would be the target. The officers who led the coup were mostly from the East, with a few Westerners. The principal victims were politicians from the North.

The North felt betrayed and revenge killings of easterners followed. A few months later, thousands of Igbos were slaughtered in the North in revenge killings and an exodus of Igbos from Northern Nigeria ensued. In response, Lt Col Emeka Ojukwu, the military governor of Eastern Nigeria, in May 1967, declared the secession and independence of the Eastern Region of Nigeria as the Republic of Biafra. The dream of a modern, strong and united Nigeria bit the dust.

With hindsight, Biafra did not stand a chance. A ferocious civil war followed and ended three years later in 1970. An estimated one million people from the old Eastern Nigeria, mostly children and the old, perished. The Nigerian army mounted an effective blockade and hundreds of thousands of children were shown on British television every night, dying from starvation. It was the first time starvation was used as a war tool in Africa. Every household in Britain had an opinion on the Biafran War. John Lennon of the Beatles handed back his OBE medal to Harold Wilson, the British prime minister, because of Britain's stand in the war.

On the battlefields, incredible acts of bravery by foreigners and easterners took place. A Swedish baron flew a Cessna aircraft with mounted machine guns as Biafra's reply to fighter jets, flown by foreigners. Fredrick Forsythe, the author, was at the war front reporting the goings-on for the BBC. He resigned from the BBC immediately after he came back from the Biafra assignment and then worked for the Biafran relief effort.

I was in charge in Liverpool in the UK of a science group of Igbos trying to get tents that could be constructed *in situ* within minutes to house refugees in the East. We raised money at meetings and we had some very good proposals. The BBC newsreader, Peter Sissons, who in those days worked for ITV as a news reporter, was badly wounded near Aba and had to be evacuated.

The Catholic charity CARITAS flew sorties of food supply planes at night, against anti-aircraft machine guns, to a road strip at Ulli, two kilometres from my village at Akokwa. For people like me who had escaped abroad, it was a nightmare. I had no news of my entire family for three years. When it ended, I had lost a lot of close friends and family relations. Nigeria has never recovered from that war.

Forty years on, in December 2001, the ruler of Akokwa, the Obi of Akokwa, Eze Osita Okoli IV conferred on me my father's chieftaincy title as the *Ihemeghonye II of Akokwa*, in recognition for my contribution to higher education in Akokwa. Life has come full circle!